YO-AJS-481

Assault on Eden

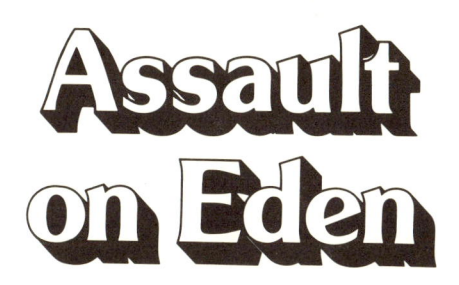

by
Eugenia Adams

William B. Eerdmans Publishing Company

ST. PHILIPS COLLEGE LIBRARY

PS
3551
.D35
A87x

Copyright © 1977 by Wm. B. Eerdmans Publishing Co.
255 Jefferson Avenue S.E., Grand Rapids, MI 49503
All rights reserved
Printed in the United States of America

Library of Congress Cataloging in Publication Data

Adams, Eugenia.
  Assault on Eden.

  I. Title.
PZ4.A2123As   [PS3551.D35]   813'.5'4   77-24656
ISBN 0-8028-1702-5

Assault on Eden

1

Now the earth was corrupt in God's sight, and the earth was filled with violence.
— Genesis 6:11

"But don't you see that all these real leaps and destructions and escapes are only attempts to get back to Eden — to something we have had, to something at least we have heard of? Don't you see one only breaks the fence or shoots the moon in order to get *home*?"
— Innocent Smith in *Manalive* by G. K. Chesterton

The sodden Kansas skies give way to the high arches of the prairie vault held up along the highway by solitary storage spires where golden grain is poured on golden grain. The heart of America is a lonely place. Few folk feel strong enough to face that kind of space and sky. Those who live there are contemptuous of the ones who eat the grain they harvest and store.

I am glad the rain has stopped, hot though it is. Perhaps the mattresses in the truck up ahead will dry out now. We roll on across the prairie, the kernel of our country. The pickup truck, twelve years old, bought for $250 from a midwestern farmer, is full of apartment-house furniture and second-hand garden tools found at auctions. High up over the cab, pointed forward like a ship's prow, is a hand plow. And the Volkswagen van I drive is full of packs and sleeping bags, seed flats and houseplants, two dogs and a big yellow cat, with the leftover arms and legs stuck in the odd crevices.

We camp that night on the outskirts of Liberal, Kansas,

in a rest area, reenacting the westward flight forty years earlier of other nameless dispossessed. But we are fleeing from affluence, not poverty. In the dark we sing around our campfire, songs of railroad men, farmers, cowboys, wanderers — lives we've never known but that draw us. We know no plaintive songs of stenographers or students, bank tellers or computer programmers. That is why we are sleeping on the hard ground of Liberal, Kansas, and waking up with dew on our faces. Like the hero in the fairy tales, we have left home to seek our fortunes. But we know none of the songs of Zion, although we have often wept by the waters of Babylon.

Indeed, we flee across the Great Plains believing the very horsemen of the apocalypse are hot on our trail. "Babylon the Great has fallen, fallen." We wonder that the people in the truck-stop cafe where we eat breakfast cannot hear the echo of that cry in the wind that blows dirt in their faces. The bodies at Kent State are barely in their graves. We are aliens in this country, in this very room. The road crew at the counter clot together over their coffee. Someone plays "Okie from Muskogee" on the juke box. We affect an ease we do not feel. Then the two groups part on the plains, we heading west, they patching the black asphalt for us to travel on, each group discussing with avid attention to detail the sociological implication of the other. "Hippies. . . ." "Hardhats. . . ."

We climb into New Mexico with relief. At last we have escaped at least affluence. The virtue of poverty engulfs us. Even the vegetation is sparse and hard-won. Dirt houses surrounded by dirt yards. Few slick Safeways and Texacos, but gas pumps with inoperable, stinking restrooms and roadside groceries. Yet out across the red raw earth are mesas of mystery floating in purple haze. A land aloof, yielding up nothing to support the glut of America.

The rise in the land is almost imperceptible to us, but not to our truck, now wheezing and balking its way up the steadily rising road. We hold our breaths and sweat. How much further, how much longer? Will we make it? Finally, the last turn, the last stretch, just at dusk. The valley has been swept by a recent cloudburst. The land is grey and pale green, and the river silver as we drop off into the valley. The wind is wet and fresh in our faces. Hope turns everything into a good omen. We park in the bare yard piled with drifts of tumbleweeds and dance around holding hands, delighted with our good fortune. We've made it back, back to our ramshackle Eden.

The reality of the place strikes us with solid force. Everything is only and exactly what it seems. No imitation carriage-house gaslight in the front yard, no aluminum-clapboard siding on the outside, no plasticized paneling on the inside. The house is adobe and no one has yet gone to the trouble of making imitation dirt.

The darkness that falls is also real, especially since the electricity has not yet been turned on. The solidity of real darkness confronts us as we search for the camping lantern and try to build a fire for supper. If the dry wood lintels stick splinters into us, what do we care? A drop of real blood oozes out, we marvel at the red beauty inside us, then wipe it carelessly, extravagantly away on our jeans.

That first night is full of strange disorientation. After we have eaten, washed the smoke from our faces, and hauled down some of the mattresses from the truck into what looks like the soundest room, we pass around a joint to take the sharp edge off our travel weariness and then crawl under the sleeping bags to await what the light will bring us. We whisper and giggle back and forth like children, listening to the mice skittering in the dark around us. Their amazement at their new tenants must almost equal ours.

My own disorientation is acute. "Where are we?" I keep asking my husband, Jack.

"In Moriah, New Mexico," he responds patiently.

"But that's just a name," I protest. "And besides, I don't know what Moriah, New Mexico *means*."

"And I don't know what *you* mean," he groans wearily. "Go to sleep. Tomorrow we'll see where we are."

"But if you don't know where you are, you're lost," I continue. This all seems terribly important to me, although I realize it only sounds dumb to everyone else.

"You're not lost," Jack says in one last effort to reassure me. "Just hold on to me. I'm here."

But where is here, I want to know, though I restrain myself from asking out loud.

Our commune, New Mexico, our new life — they are all only a place in our heads. Is it the same place where we lie tonight? Do our minds' map and the land match?

I lie in the unfamiliar darkness and feel the mattress under us like a ship unmoored, drifting away. We are moving through the night, towards what dark shore none of us knows. *This* is what Robinson Crusoe felt. This is the meaning of shipwreck, not knowing where you are. I cling tightly to Jack. Jack is a place I know. There is at least a foothold here.

One thing is certain. There is no going back. What makes people do crazy things like this? Some have broken with their families, rejected their educations, given up jobs of at least a modicum of prestige and security. It is no small act to have come this far, wherever it is.

Those who glibly speak of "copping out" (called come-outerism in the nineteenth century) little know the desperation of those driven into the wilderness during this time. It is escape from certain danger into the unknown. But as Tolkien said, the only one who despises escape is a jailor. One might as well have tried to persuade Noah to leave off building the ark and run for city councilman or set up a mental health clinic in Antedeluvia as to talk to us about reforming the system from within. Noah and we are political realists. No doubt "cop out" was one of the primeval epithets that assaulted the ark-builder, and we are equally oblivious to it. Let the fools beat their bourgeois brains out against the crumbling wall of reform. Somehow they all end up wearing the same clothes and carrying the same credit cards as the oppressors. The mark of the beast, as far as we are concerned, is dispensed by IBM computer printouts.

Apocalypse, apocalypse. How often it is in our mouths. The end, doom, destruction. Wrath and justice are once again combined for us with the same alchemy that kindled the hot desire for vindication in the captive Jews and the Christians under Domitian. We have a horror of violence and will not ourselves aid the destruction of a system doomed to fall under its own weight of evil, but neither do we intend to stand in the way of any scourge of God. We cheer on the avenging angel.

All America is, in the summer of 1970, in the same sad shape as the "burned-over district" of New York state in the 1820's.

> Socialistic and communitarian theories reinforced literalistic concern for the early Christian communism described in the New Testament (Acts 2:41-47). Mysticism and various forms of pantheism provided links to important philosophic trends of the time. Other interests, often with only remote Christian rootage or none at all, kept appearing and reappearing in different contexts. The discovery and popularization of "animal magnetism" (hypnotism) added a new dimension to popular conceptions of human consciousness. Lurking under America's puritanic Victorianism was a persistent and not sufficiently appreciated restiveness about sex and the monogamous family. . . .
> (Sydney E. Ahlstrom, *A Religious History of the American People*, p. 477)

This heritage of the insatiable religious quest burns in our American bones. A century and a half later, the refurbished panaceas of religious gurus are still considered entertaining enough for prime-time television.

The historical undercurrents of our own experiment come from many tributaries, most of which we are ignorant of. For instance, there is something of Joseph Smith and Nauvoo in our midst. If we cannot swallow the unsophisticated Book of Mormon, neither can we let go that dark and bloody irrationalism that fosters paranoia and persecution. We too have our own "special revelations," whether they be

Edgar Cayce or Paul Ehrlich. Whether one uses the mystic or the scientific metaphor, it makes little difference. All signs point toward The End. We all expect the disintegration of American society and that it will be in one way or another violent. Our one hope is that there will be a saving remnant and we will be a part of that. "I am like a huge, rough stone," proclaimed Joseph Smith,

> rolling down from a high mountain; and the only polishing I get is when some corner gets rubbed off by coming in contact with something else, striking with accelerated force against religious bigotry, priestcraft, lawyer-craft, doctor-craft, lying editors, suborned judges and jurors, and the authority of perjured executives, backed by mobs, blasphemers, licentious and corrupt men and women — all hell knocking off a corner here and a corner there. Thus will I become a polished shaft in the quiver of the Almighty, who will give me dominion over all and every one of them, when their refuge of lies shall fail, and their hiding place shall be destroyed.

But there is also more than a bit of Brook Farm in us. The educated's love of discourse: problematic, hypothetical, analytical. The "Plan of the West Roxbury Community," published in that nineteenth-century voice of the avant garde, *The Dial,* in January of 1842, could have come hot off the underground press of 1970, except for a few genteel curlicues here and there, and could easily have gained the unanimous approval of our group:

> A few individuals, who, unknown to each other, under different disciplines of life, reacting from different social evils, but aiming at the same object — of being wholly true to their natures as men and women; have been made acquainted with one another, and have determined to become the Faculty of the Embryo University.
>
> In order to live a religious and moral life worthy the name, they feel it is necessary to come out in some degree from the world, and to form themselves into a community of property, so far as to exclude competition and the ordinary rules of trade. . . . They have bought a farm, in order to make agriculture the basis of their life, it being the most direct and simple in relation to nature.
>
> A true life, although it aims beyond the highest star, is redo-

lent of the healthy earth. The perfume of clover lingers about it. The lowing of cattle is the natural bass to the melody of human voices. . . .

The community aims to be rich, not in the metallic representative of wealth, but in the wealth itself, which money should represent; namely, LEISURE TO LIVE IN ALL THE FACULTIES OF THE SOUL.

High-flown sentiments, it is easy enough to say in ridicule. The natural bass of the lowing cattle lost its charm when Hawthorne confronted the manure pile, about which the perfume of clover decidedly did not linger. But after the dream has dwindled through ridicule, think how powerful the compulsion must be to drive people to stake their lives on such a slender spider web of a dream. All the history made in America was by such desperate people wagering upon a desperate dream.

Like the Faculty of the Embryo University, most of us have at least some college education. What kind of culture is it that offers openhandedly the best fruits of its civilization only to have them spurned? Many among us could never have read the books we have or ingested our ideas in any other time or place. But if one has "every opportunity," the opportunity one chooses is likely to be the unlikely, the unusual. Joseph Smith, uneducated and unpropertied, had not had every opportunity. Like a water course bursting through the only narrow opening available to it, his movement was swift and strong. But the folks at Brook Farm came and went, discussing Kant and Transcendentalism, notions much too evanescent for the "King of the Kingdom of God." The summer of 1844 saw the martyring of the Mormons and the dwindling of Brook Farm, just as the summer of 1970 saw the Kent State deaths and the withering of flower power.

Perhaps not religion but education is the opiate of the people. Who will die for philosophical speculation? Not even Galileo.

Like the Brook Farmers, we too are dilettantes. They

dabbled in the Shakers and the Rappites; we stock our library with Zen and Baba Ram Dass.

What a sad hybrid we are! For whatever our affinities with Brook Farm, that experiment aimed at being a utopia, while we will settle for nothing short of paradise. Utopias bore us. There is no mighty vindication, no justice and wrath in the coming of a Utopia, only a "re-education." Give us a good, resounding apocalypse, full of the crashes of capitalism, the wailing and gnashing of Nixon's teeth, the fumes of the military-industrial complex rising like incense. And then. . . . The picture dissolves, the transition is unclear, but suddenly there we are: innocent, strong, loving. Every step in harmony with the great cosmic dance. A delirious vision we are all devoted to. It is no great concern that the transition is unclear. Like all good children brought up on Walt Disney, we believe that if you wish for something hard enough, it is bound to come true. At present we are only interested in the first vision. Paradise will have to wait till tomorrow.

But tomorrow does come, and in the light of morning our paradise seems to be disguised as a desert, made green only here and there in strips of irrigated alfalfa and in need of quite a few repairs. Crumbling adobe sifts down through the cracking plaster. Windows are broken out. Judging from the eroded walls, the roof leaks in many places.

Still, opening our eyes to a sun whose light is more immediately present than we are used to is intoxicating. It has already climbed over the mesa that lies to the east of our house, and the rest of the world — insects, birds, air currents, even the solitary neighboring farmer, each with its own particular phototropism — is responding to the light. Eager to become a part of this busy, buzzing natural world, we hurry outside, stretch and yawn broadly, and begin unloading the truck and van.

New ventures, though, are never propelled only by a corporate vision, I think. There must be that if ever a group of people are to act together, but who knows what private yearnings held the people individually to that stake in Nauvoo or kept even the dilettantes at Brook Farm for their season's stay? We have Hawthorne's account in *The Blithedale Romance* of his observations of certain characters, including his own, in this romantic and tragic interlude. Though they all ascribe openly to that intoxicating dream of "brotherhood," each one has some secret, sometimes even from themselves, reason for acting out the dream: ambition, pride, guilt, desire to be loved, to foster a family, to be provided with an identity.

And we are no different. Amongst the bundles, the bedding, the furniture, the garden tools and the pets, we have brought with us the hidden desires, the private dreams. We want Paradise in the particular. Our own Adam or Eve, a picture of a bower carried around in our pockets and saved for years, plans for ways to fill our days.

Faye, for example, who sings almost constantly, plays the flute around the campfire at night, and shuffles around in a queer, private dance, is voracious for excitement. Some interior drama, like her dance, accompanies her everywhere, preparing a role for every situation. She even buys dramatically outdated clothes at thrift stores to dress up for her part. This westward-moving caravan, leaving the island of the university campus just as it has been closed by the student strike, is exactly the thing to capture her imagination. A hundred years earlier she would have been a dance hall girl, a riverboat gambler, an explorer, Mother Ann Lee. Now she is Faye, girl-communitarian, free spirit, hitchhiker.

If Faye is seeking excitement, Wayne is seeking security. Where she branches out, he wants to take root. He's not a drifter, but a settler. This venture provides him with a place to settle, to build on, build up, work, care for. Broad-shouldered and brooding, he also needs someone to work and care for, someone to share his vision with. A most unwieldy combination of old-fashioned, homespun virtues in a culture where they only work in TV westerns. So to counter that culture, he has joined up with this new settlement. Maybe this is the place where he can get on with his dream.

Sally is a bright young career girl who can find no meaningful career in straight society. Independent and creative, she would ideally like a loom, a weaving shop. Friends she can rely on. A surrogate family in which her childlike whimsies can have full play. Where there are children to whom she can tell her funny little stories, peopled with creatures from her imagination. She makes up adventurous life histories for all our pets and adds to them weekly. But her spirit has been worn dangerously thin in places. She, Faye, and Wayne have all lost their fathers, Sally only recently. For her the wound is still fresh. She is illness-prone, and many of us feel an unvoiced dread that Sally, tough and resilient as she seems, is the most vulnerable among us to whatever malevolent spirits lurk about.

If Thoreau went to the woods to catch life by the throat and force from it its secrets, Daniel has inherited his hero's analytic desires. Like his nineteenth-century mentor, he is unencumbered with personal involvements that get in the way of his experiments with life. Trained as an architect, he has already been both in the Peace Corps in the Far East and in the army in Korea. Now is the time to explore "alternative lifestyles." He wants to discover, in the classical sense, "the way to live." Not impulsive or romantic like the rest of us, he seeks order, balance.

Lillian is quite purposively starting a new life. Her divorce has recently been granted. An academic career and a marriage to which she has given six years of her life have just disintegrated. She is determined that she has worn out her last rut. A new life, one shaped by her own quite capable hands, something daring and decidedly un-mousey, is what she wants. And other people around to keep up one's spirits. But never again a dependency on a person who can betray her. Lillian has only just discovered that the world is full of cabbages and kings and she means to explore them all.

This is only a sample of the personal needs brought into the fifty arid acres and the ramshackle adobe farm house. Sometimes there were as many as seventeen secret worlds bumping up against one another there. And who knows what other unspoken yearnings drove people — young, intelligent, educated, with every advantage their parents dreamed of — into the desert to take up a barbaric life? In a way, the public, corporate articulations of our goals, couched primarily in political rhetoric, were an amalgam of all the private disappointments with life in mainstream society.

Like Noah, we lived amongst violence. There was no excitement but in violence, no peace or place to settle in unreasoning and virulent family scenes, disorder and imbalance, desertion, despair. The more mythic elements of our country's violence were being exported to a foreign setting in Vietnam to be staged for the daily television ritual. It was this violence, on every level, that we sought to flee. Yet it was not the ark we wanted to build, that small, stifling temporary place of waiting for the fulfillment of the promise. We were impatient for Paradise. And ignoring the cherubim and the flaming sword, we plotted to storm the gates of Eden.

2

> And the eyes of the two were opened, and they knew that they were naked.
> — Genesis 3:7

> If the jewel which every one desired to possess lay far out on a frozen lake where the ice was very thin, watched over by the danger of death, while, closer in, the ice was perfectly safe, then in a passionate age the crowds would applaud the courage of the man who ventured out. . . . But in an age without passion, in a reflective age, it would be otherwise. People would think each other clever in agreeing that it was unreasonable and not even worth while to venture out so far.
> — Kierkegaard, *The Present Age*

July 4, 1970. We start off the day playing the Hallelujah Chorus into the sleeping ear of Bob, whose birthday it is. Everyone is struck by the irony of the situation. The birthday of the country we both love and hate. Bob's birthday. Bob's father is a U.S. senator.

Bob is only recently out of a mental hospital where he spent his adolescence. Being anti-social, that is, preferring animals to people, he was an embarrassment to his father's political career. Bob has a big orange cat without a tail who tolerates only Bob touching him. The cat catches rabbits in the night and we hear them scream.

I am puzzled at why Bob was diagnosed as anti-social, although he confirms that at the time it was an accurate description. He is more rarely morose than any of us. He is both talkative and articulate. He sometimes worries about his relationship to women, but he is after all only eighteen today. Spoiled by too much money. His brain perhaps a little wacky from incredible amounts of home-brew drugs concocted in the hospital. He can recite entire albums of Firesign Theatre. We are all exasperated by him, yet dote on him.

Everything moves like molasses in the mornings. Discipline is a dirty word in this crumbling adobe house, built by some unknown Spanish/Indian before the land it sits on ever became a part of the country whose birthday, along with Bob's, we are gradually gearing up to celebrate. Its present inhabitants use incomprehensibly stupid phrases like "doing my own thing" in a six-room house that holds from seven to eighteen people, has no bathroom, a leaky roof, broken windows, and one cold-water spigot whose source no one checks the purity of and which eventually gives us all paratyphoid.

No one enjoys the chaos and disorder and dirt. We are all more or less uncomfortable with it. Yet some secretly know that this is for them only temporary, and they escape the panic the rest of us feel over the huge droning flies and the crud that creeps further from the corner of the kitchen daily.

Finally things coalesce enough to get breakfast fixed. Ninety-five percent of the cooking is done by the women; the other five percent by Bob, who enjoys making his specialty dishes. Another example of the astounding gap between rhetoric and reality that none of us is prepared to deal with.

Bob's honorary breakfast is served in bed. He gets toast and eggs. The rest of us eat boiled brown wheat berries, part of the hundred-pound sack we bought on our way through Kansas to New Mexico. They are hard to cook and hard to eat, but no one complains. First, everyone is constantly hungry. And then this is a contact with reality we all share. Everyone's teeth are grinding away on those indomitable grains, soaking in the thin dry milk and honey.

No one would exchange his bowl for one of Sugar Snacks, but we all envy Bob his eggs.

By the time the dishes have been sulked over by whoever turn it is (dishwashing is our sole attempt at a work schedule), it is almost noon, and we turn to the celebration of the day. Imported by our latest midwestern immigrant are ten caps of psylocibin. As always there are intricate details to be worked out with great care, many of them ethical questions. In this there is no floundering: there are no outside experts, there is no appeal to authority other than the seniority within our own group. We are the authorities, and we approach the subject vigorously.

Should everyone drop? At the same time? Should it be allotted according to body weight, tolerance, or request? Should we all stay together? Who will look after any problems that develop? Who will deal with outsiders, should they appear? What about the two children?

As it turns out, we drop at staggered times. A couple of people don't drop at all, so there is plenty to go around, all of us taking what we decide we can handle.

It is only around psychedelics that we become a true community, even tribal. There is never any hoarding of dope. We never are floating in the stuff, but whatever there is is shared among us all. It is the basis of most of our celebrations — like cocktail parties, only homelier. It clarifies our rift with society, thus drawing us, despite our other failures, closer together. If we have to choose between us and them, we know what our choice will be.

There is some concern about the quality of the psylocibin, which after all is not covered by the FDA, so a few of the hardiest go first to try it out. The women are whipping up covered dishes for the final event of the day — a picnic on the rocks and cliff down by the river. By one o'clock everyone has ingested at least half a cap of psylocibin and we start for the river, half a mile away.

The sonorro, over which in innocent awe we continually wander, both stoned and straight, is the best of our lives here. In it we are closest to realizing what we have come here for. Here — outside the society we have fled, outside ourselves — is a world of such integrity and harmony that we stumble along, fondling the rocks, smelling the juniper, waiting for a message, sure that if we have a home on this earth, we would like it to be the way the stones here have homes. As soon as we cross the irrigation ditch in front of the house there is half a mile of unbroken silence and sun to the river over a ground whose holiness we do not understand but sense. Our stupidity lessens and we listen.

Somehow we have managed to stray from one another and are now scattered in small clusters across the sonorro. I have a flash of how incongruous we would look to a passing helicopter. The chemicals have begun to clamp down; it descends with a rush, that feeling of lack of control, so intriguing to the Western mind. Something else is in control — karma, the desert, God. We don't really know, but we are sure it's not ourselves. We wait to see where, literally, the spirit will move us.

The two of us are at the sandy bottom of an arroyo beside a big cottonwood. I have two problems to work on: the constant nausea produced by the chemicals and the way the lines in the rocks keep becoming snakes. Not that I am afraid of them. I simply realize that there is a practical necessity to be able to distinguish the rock-snakes from real-snakes. We feel close and comfortable in our small oasis. Jack says not to worry, that he will take care of me. I believe him. We make love at the foot of the cottonwood, both from sheer delight in one another and because we've read it is impossible under these conditions.

Afterwards there is the now gigantic task before us of getting to the river. It seems that as soon as we get settled in one place, there is always the irritation of having to move on. We realize that our perspective has shifted, that it is objectively no more than a ten-minute walk to the river. Yet it has assumed the proportions of a trail drive across the plains. It is Christopher Robin's expedition to the North

Pole. This double vision amuses us greatly, yet our amusement does not evaporate the huge reality. The shade of the tree shifts over the sand as the wind blows, replacing shadow with light and back again. It all seems a marvel. We talk about our parents, how our love for them and theirs for us is somehow missing a vital connection. It all seems a great waste. A tangible wave of pity sweeps over us and we cry for a while. Then it seems time to move on.

Out from under the dappled shade of the cottonwood, down through the arroyo, stained purple and gold and pale green. The colors are real, part of the audacity of the desert. The patterns they make are the games our minds are playing with us. We climb the soft side of the arroyo onto the top of the plain again, picking our way among the rock and cactus, concentrating hard on avoiding the spikes of Spanish sword that stud this vast fakir's couch. Up ahead is a high knoll where others are already scrambling at various levels. Gradually everyone is converging on this high point from which we can see the flood plain, a village a few miles away, our own house behind us, and overhead a hawk wheeling.

There is some small panic, scrambling to the top of the rocks. My bone-deep desire to stay put in one place, not to have to move again, is in constant tension with the flow going on around me. Necessity — to stay with the others, to get to the place of meeting, to be where the food is at the right time — necessity inexorably drives us on, when I want so desperately to be still. There is partial satisfaction in each way station of the trip, but what I long for is reaching a place I won't have to move from. I know that once I get to the top of the knoll, there will be another resting place. I won't have to move again at least for a while. Therefore, bridging the gap between where I am now and the place I want to be makes the desire to compress time acute. I want to *already* be there. The seconds to the top seem interminable, but finally we are there and again in the midst of our friends. It seems a very long time since we last saw them, and everyone is full of congratulations for each other on the success of the trip so far.

Some people are examining marks on the rocks they think are Indian petroglyphs. Bob begins to make up an elaborate tale about how they came to be there. He is only a little wackier stoned than straight. I lean back against a dark granite boulder, fighting off nausea and thinking how crazy we all are. Yet it doesn't seem at all unnatural.

Later, when we have all scrambled down on the far side of the rocks and descended into the riverbed itself, Jack and I wander upstream around a bend. The river is low, only ankle deep in most places. We marvel at the smooth, water-worn stones, the way they fit the curve of the water. The wet satiny sand gives way softly beneath our feet. A big boulder further upstream looks like the prow of a ship sticking up out of the water. It becomes another way station in my mind, like the cottonwood tree and the top of the rocky knoll, where I can rest for a while. We wade out to it and I crawl up on top and lie back with relief. After I assure Jack that I will be all right alone for a while, he goes off on some private exploration.

The silence and the water lap up around my rock. Overhead in the gap of tremulous blue sky left by the cliff walls which rise sharply on both sides of the river here, the clouds move by. Clouds such as I have never seen them before. It is not the old game of seeing shapes in clouds, which tends to flatten them out against a background. Strangely, it never occurs to me to see them that way today. For what I am most keenly aware of is the depth, the dimensions of the clouds. They do not sail along like ships with a stable top and bottom, but they roll and tumble in wide, slow arcs as they move across the roof of the canyon. Nor do they coagulate and disperse into wisps. There is merely a certain spectrum of light in which they are visible to our eyes and they move in and out through that spectrum. This is quite clear to me. When they reach a certain height or depth they simply fade through the limits of my perception, like the Cheshire cat disappearing bit by bit, only to reappear when once again they roll up into the, for me, proper spectrum.

It is the purest, most fascinating spectacle I have ever witnessed. I could watch forever and never grow tired. Not only is the sight all any heart could have hoped for, the kind of thing movies are always leading up to but never quite bring off, the wholly undisappointably magnificent, but also I am quite sure that up on the level where the clouds are turning and tumbling in fantastic spirals and pirouettes, there is music they are dancing to. Stately, majestic cloud-music that I can almost hear, can even feel the vibrations of tingling my ears. The best of all is that I know there are no gimmicks and there is no end. There will be no hint of shoddiness around the edges, no "That's all folks!" written across the sky, no list of credits, and the clouds will continue to dance whether or not anyone is there to watch them. This is infinitely satisfying.

When at last Jack returns and says it is time we started moving back downstream where the others are, I am still so fascinated by the clouds that I am mildly impatient with anything that takes my attention away from them. I would have liked to make the trip floating on my back so as not to miss any of the high spectacle. As it is, the best I can do is insist that we stop every few yards to see to what point they have progressed.

We make one long stop beside a grassy bank where a seep spring trickles down into the river. This land is full of surprises. Dry, overgrazed for years, its chalky bones exposed daily to the domineering sun, it does offer a few tucked-away secret spots where enough water collects to make familiar green life possible. Along the trickle are lush emerald grass and even tiny flowers. A few feet below, the red raw river runs. Up above, the sonorro bakes in the sun. And here, in an out-of-the-way wrinkle, is a miniature meadow.

As we sit gazing down the river, we see a figure leaping

and zigzagging back and forth across a broad sandbar. Her hair is flying out behind her as she laughs and splashes. We come closer and see that it is our ten-year-old, playing at being a river-sprite. We sit on our heels and watch her, dancing as the clouds danced, something entirely outside ourselves. She has tied onto herself every available colored scarf she could find at the house, and now she is making them all flutter and dance around her like feathers and flames. I feel a relief much like the one I felt about the clouds. Just as they would continue their solemn rolling way across the sky whether I was there or not, so she would exist, be a person, with or without me. If this sounds like a desire to be quit of responsibility, it is not. I definitely *do* want to be there, just as I wanted to go on watching the clouds forever. I simply realize at this moment that I do not hold this person in existence. Some other power outside of me makes her tie colored scarves to her brown little body and dance by the river. I am only background, like the sky to the clouds.

    We come out of our hiding place and she calls to us to hurry. The picnic is ready now. Indeed the afternoon is stretching thin out across the flood plain. It has been several hours since we left the house. We take a path up from the river onto a high, flat cliff that extends precariously over the water. Back away from the eroded cliff edge in the ruins of an adobe hut, built and abandoned by an unknown settler, the food is spread out. A black iron pot of beans, a casserole full of rice spiked with whatever tidbits could be found in the kitchen, a sesame cake, tortillas, salad from our meager garden, and Kool-aid. Everyone is in good spirits. The scene reminds me, incongruously enough, of church picnics, fishing camps by the river, family reunions. It is much closer to these than to the backyard barbeques of the suburbs. A regular old-fashioned Fourth of July. And then as the sun falls and our campfire lights up our faces, it is more like being refugees, stopping for a while on a long trek to an unknown destination. The darkness is close and comfortable.

For several days Bob had been working on some special fireworks for the occasion. Explosives had been part of his antisocial behavior, starting with his first junior chemistry set. After everyone has eaten and settled back into the midsummer darkness, he sets up his display, a series of rockets aimed out across the river to the sandy flood plain far down on the other side. They are big and noisy but haven't the colored showers of sparks I had been hoping for. When they are spent, we discover our own makeshift variety. Setting fire to the ends of driftwood sticks, we twirl them in patterns through the black velvet night. The glowing ends make pale colored streaks that seem to hang in the air like whirling wheels. When the dervish operating the stick gets wound up enough, he flings it flaming out across the arching sky to the river, making a long luminous rainbow in the night. The colors linger long enough, at least on our retinas, for everyone to exhale a long ahhh at the spectacle. Some of us simply sit and watch as others develop more and more complicated patterns. This is real fireworks.

At last someone realizes that it is getting too cold to stay up on the cliff much longer. When the sun goes down behind the foothills the heat drains quickly from the desert. We collect the pots and pans and start the trek back to the house.

Half a mile across a sonorro at night is quite different from the same distance by day. The moon has risen like a giant floodlight, making the plain below into an immense stage setting. We wander up and over rises, into and down arroyos, scrambling up the sides again. On one comparatively flat place we pause for a trucking demonstration. Trucking, that inexplicably hilarious comic-book walk, somewhat akin to a vaudeville stroll, is meant to accentuate our absurdity in the world. One leans as far back as gravity allows and reaches gingerly forward with each foot, pumping the arms in time. Some among us have developed it to the point of art, like Charlie Chaplin's penguin waddle.

The way we see our place in the world is always through the filter of movies or comic strips. Nature we can take straight. Its coherence and integrity is so great as to command even our desiccated sense of respect and awe. We can simply sit quietly and look, but all the time knowing that we ourselves do not participate in that coherence and integrity. We can only be observers. The moment we move or open our mouths, our outsideness, our not-knowing-how-to-be rises up and overcomes us. So it is not without significance that we translate ourselves into comic book characters, doing our funny, futile dance across the desert. Incongruity is all we really understand.

I am getting very tired, worried that someone is going to get lost and be left behind in that endless maze of ravines. (That and stepping on cactus is all any of us is ever afraid of there, however, so much is it like a vast, endlessly amusing playground.) I begin to doubt that we will ever make it back; we will go on wandering forever among the rocks like the Israelites without a Moses. The longing for rest, for home, for a place to stay becomes physically acute, and I have to work hard on controlling my panic and anguish.

Strangely, no one gets lost, and soon we come up over the last hump that is the downward side of the irrigation canal. Walking along it single file, we smell the heavy night fragrance of the sacred datura bushes blooming there, the native psychedelic used in past ages by the Indians but alien to us. We tramp noisily across the wooden bridge and are home.

As we enter the glaring electric blaze of the house, the magic of the desert and the river clang down behind us. It is like passing a physical barrier.

The two children are caked with mud. One of them has indeed gotten a cactus thorn in her foot. The euphoria is gone, but the physical effects that become handicaps when something must be done remain. Assembling soap and water and towel, scrubbing away the mud, disinfecting the cut, are all tasks requiring great effort and concentration. Everyone else has dumped the dirty dishes in the kitchen and disappeared into the dining room-library to talk off the rest of the chemicals. I feel angry and deserted. As I sit in the kitchen looking at the spills on the impossible concrete floor, feeling the food drying and caking in the dishes around me, the quintessence of the despair all housewives feel at the inevitable cyclical drudgery of their lives settles over me. The voices from the other room surge with laughter.

Finally the children are bathed and sent to bed. I creep out the sagging screen door and down the line of windows and doors to the large stone room I share with Jack. I know everyone else is sitting around the big oak table — *my* big oak table — eulogizing the day and themselves. How great it was to be in the midst of nature, to be really living, to be surrounded by such caring comrades. I know they are all lying, and I want them to realize it. To taste as bitterly as I do the deceit of their words. Not only the casual and literal dumping of their responsibility, but the lies they continue to tell themselves, their self-congratulation. Certainly they don't care about me. And how could they? They don't even know me. My depression and self-pity are gargantuan. Someone comes to the door and I growl at the figure to go away.

I want desperately to escape into sleep, but it will be hours before the motor that has become my mind will slow its racing enough for that. I pace back and forth. Sit and stare at the rough concrete wall that shapes and reshapes itself into maps of unknown worlds, each indentation a continental shelf.

I know, with one part of my mind, that this will end eventually. Yet with the part of me that feels time, it seems it will never end. I am caught in a time trap, a cage through whose bars I can look out and see tomorrow and myself released and in control again but which freedom I cannot reach at this moment.

I cry and rage and hate until even that emotional pool is drained dry. And still all I can do is wait. Wait. Empty and dry and despairing. Separated not only from the desert, the rocks, the cottonwood tree, and the clouds, but from the human figures around me. My thoughts, I know, would be alien and shocking to them, still riding on that shimmering wave of optimism and good feeling. I am so weary and long for rest. Obliteration would have been welcome, simply to disappear into the dark night, dropping beyond memory, without a soul.

3

> And I will put enmity between you and the woman, and between your offspring and her offspring; he shall crush your head and you shall snap at his heel.
> — Genesis 3:15

> To be brief, therefore, let the readers know, that they have then truly apprehended by faith what is meant by God being the Creator of heaven and earth, if they, in the first place, follow this universal rule, not to pass over, with ungrateful inattention or oblivion, those glorious perfections which God manifests in his creatures, and, secondly learn to make such an application to themselves as thoroughly to affect their hearts.
> — Calvin, *Institutes,* I, xiv, 21

Bob was supposedly anti-social and obsessively attached to his cat Rusty. But Rusty was only one of our many pets. Different dogs ran under our feet at various stages of this history. These pets were only shadows of ourselves, almost like well-worn teddy bears that served whatever function the specific situation called for. There was Dina, a badly beaten and undernourished German shepherd someone of us had rescued, who licked everyone compulsively. Paris, a runt Weimarraunner, also neurotic, who fortunately disappeared several months after our arrival. Pucci, another foundling, short, curly and evil-tempered, lost in the streets of town. Phoebe Zeitgeist, a kitten actually born at Moriah who was taken off by one of our emigrés. Her brother, Chef Boyardee, who, while exploring the roof one day, fell through the stove pipe opening to a gruesome death in the ashes below. And Jennifer, an adolescent Airedale of the latter era who refused to be housebroken.

None of these animals provided us with anything but a mirror. To confront animal life, I discover now, it is necessary to deal with something other than pets. We were the downfall of our dogs; whatever souls they had were distorted by contact with us.

Of course, there was no clear idea then of confronting a type of life different from our own to see what mysteries it would open to us. But in a hazy, surburban-starved way we knew animals were special, could tell us something. Thus many of us were eager to "get into animals," as we so clumsily put it, some because animal husbandry seemed more interesting than hoeing corn, some because it seemed more masculine, some from the desire to domesticate. Who knows all the reasons?

At any rate, our first animal acquisitions were, safely enough, rabbits. Lillian brought them out on the train all the way from Missouri. Four white, not quite grown rabbits. We hurried them home to the farm, put them in the dilapidated cages that our nameless precursor had used, opened our brand new sack of rabbit pellets, filled the water dishes, and waited. The rabbits only stared back from their strange pink eyes. They would have been a lesson in passive resistance and guerrilla tactics had we had the sense enough to observe that. As soon as we fed them and had had our fill of staring and left them alone, they immediately began chewing through the chicken wire, the wood frames, any destructible part of their cage.

It was a constant battle, keeping the rabbits in. We would go out to feed them in the mornings, only to find the entire herd furtively munching away the lettuce patch. An hour's chase ensued, the human predators trying to entrap the small darting figures before the dogs could fall upon them.

For every new litter of babies there was a corresponding new disease to keep the population stable. Our visions of a rabbit farm began to dim. Buying expensive feed, cutting alfalfa by hand, cleaning cages, doing makeshift repairs on hutches. Twice a day attendance with the water pail. In this way the prey wreaks the revenge of the parasite.

And always the rabbits resisted us. One could count on several long red scratches for each transfer of a rabbit from one cage to another — for mating, for kindling, for the never ending repairs. If we handled the babies, we inevitably found the stiff little body on the ground the next morning. Our rabbits had a strong sense of ritual purity.

Once we began collecting rabbits, they seemed to pour in from all our Chicano neighbors who must have already recognized their folly. Thus our herd grew, not so much from reproduction as from rejection.

Our suburban sensibilities disturbed by the incarceration of creatures in hutches, we finally tried making a rabbit yard, fenced in with a shed for shelter, in order to more closely approximate their natural habitat. We had reckoned without their natural territorial imperatives, however. The males fought ferociously and had to be put back in isolation. The does and babies co-existed fairly peaceably, but their escape instinct did not subside. The hard red clay that was like stone to our garden tools, yielded to their sharp toenails like loam. Elaborate tunnels appeared overnight from the shed to the outside world.

Once, after our herd had been pretty well depleted of breedable stock, I heard of a family in the next village who was selling its rabbits. Simon and I loaded a refrigerator-size cardboard box on the back of the truck and started off to find this bargain. A cold wind full of dirt was whipping at the weak winter light as we bumped along the back roads, trying to follow our sketchy directions to the Villanuevas. Finally we ferreted out the right house and inquired at the door. The woman who answered listened to us stoney-faced and then referred us without comment to her son who had just come home from school.

The Villanueva rabbit enterprise had deteriorated even more than ours. The boy had kept the rabbits for a 4-H project, now fortunately behind him. The rabbit reticence had almost gone out of these creatures. Instead of guerrillas, they were near to open combat with their keepers. Loose in even a larger pen than ours, they were only tossed occasional batches of hay and watered in rusty hubcaps. Their burrows in the sand were worthy of wild rabbits, and probably all that kept them from escape were the equally half-wild dogs that blinked at them from the other side of the fence.

The boy, with evident relief that this was his last bout with his adversaries, entered the cage and began throwing himself upon them with a rage that only springs from retribution. The rabbits scattered screaming. Gradually he closed in on each one, lunging after them, catching their hind legs and throwing them in high arcs, their long lean bodies struggling against the dirty wind, into the box on the truck bed.

When it was over, he brushed at the dirt that covered him, left the cage door hanging on its hinges in the wind, and accepted our money the way a conqueror accepts tribute.

After a year and a half of rabbit handling, the last few months of which were filled with stringy rabbit stews, the sole survivor of this experiment was a sickly white angora called Furball. His eyes were constantly infected; he had refused to breed with any of the does we tempted him with; he would even allow himself to be cuddled by the children. Lacking the requisite ruthlessness of real nomads, we carted Furball and his unwieldy cage around for three more moves after we left the farm, finally disposing of him in much the same manner he had been dumped on us.

Late in our first fall we decided to branch out into larger animals. Being politically adverse to cows, which after all were responsible for the deplorably overgrazed condition of this part of the country, we decided on goats. All the homesteading books and magazines recommended these creatures as clean, intelligent, easily maintained, and productive.

Again Simon and I in the pickup started over the mountains to a retirement village a hundred miles away where, we had heard, some goats were for sale. The day was bright and beautiful, and the lush mountain meadows that flourished in what had once been volcanic craters filled our hearts with dreams — sleek, frisky creatures drowning us with their rich milk. The day seemed a better portent than the occasion of our rabbit venture.

We reached the village, found out our goat-lady, and began the long bargaining process. Many retirees, from the security of their pensions and odd jobs, doted on hippies, indeed, almost made them their hobby. Particularly the naturopathically inclined who thrived on yeast and lecithin. In this woman's trailer were boxes containing tiny wheat farms in various stages of sprouting. She fed it to her cats and also munched handfuls herself. Outside were the remains of a garden truly to be proud of, with such exotics as Jerusalem artichokes, the roots of which she insisted upon digging up for us to plant in our own patch.

"Absolutely no trouble at all," she assured us. "Just stick 'em in the ground and next year you'll have these great big sunflower-type plants," she gestured the predicted height above her head, "and underneath these little yellow potato-like things." We gratefully accepted the free sample with visions of a full root cellar next year.

Everything the woman touched, eccentric and talkative as she was, seemed to thrive: her miniature indoor wheat farms, her garden, her apple trees, and most of all her goats. They behaved with admirable goat-like energy. She demonstrated the milk which came in vigorous squirts into the plastic pail. We sampled and were sold. We took a full-grown white female of breedable age and a Nubian adolescent female ready to breed in six more months. Into the truck they went after many promises on our part to give them a good home and instructions on her part of what that entailed.

The drive home was somewhat less ideal than the

morning trip had been. Weekend traffic out of Albuquerque piled up around us. The truck began to overheat and make strange noises. As the darkness fell I developed fears of leading two strange goats down the highway in the cold with no hope of hitchhiking. We managed to limp home, though, and unload the frightened, indignant animals in the dark.

The next day began a more serious enslavement than the rabbits had ever meant. They at least had been ostensibly passive; the goats were openly aggressive. Maisie, the older white one, never ever agreed with us about anything. During a week-long visit, she did manage to get impregnated by a billy belonging to friends who lived fifty miles away. And she did, in the course of time, bring forth two lovely golden kids who doubled the amount of time we spent mending the fence. But only in those ways did she follow the book. She did not produce the predicted gallons of milk. What we did squeeze out of her she generally managed to kick over, despite our attempts to follow the best milking techniques in the book.

Matilda was another matter. She was a picture-book goat, frisky and mischievous. She danced and cavorted, was wilful and unpredictable. But picturesqueness was about all she supplied. And as she became larger and stronger, and her cavorting harder to control, her charms, like those of a precocious spoiled child, began to pale.

Still we kept up the cult, milking twice a day, determined to strip the last drop from the recalcitrant teat, pouring over the 1931 Farm Bureau pamphlets, resolved to make it work, bewildered as to why it didn't. We read of success after success in *Mother Earth News* and *Organic Gardening* and grew more ashamed of our own failure.

The birth of the kids the next year offered some relief from our discouragement. We all sat hunkered in the goat stall or on top of the fence watching something actually happening. The quivering gelatinous balloons slowly emerged as Maisie panted and strained at her work, intent and oblivious to us. The delicate little hooves had never yet touched earth. The silky ears took shape before our eyes as the mother licked them clean. It was a miracle that they moved, that they were real. Finally something had turned out the way it should, the way it had been promised.

With four goats quartered near the garden, it was necessary to have them carefully watched during the day when they grazed. Jane, the youngest child and unburdened with school, got the job, not one she disliked, for of all of us, Jane was closest to the animals. She was still, in a way, one of them. She didn't hold their uncooperativeness against them. She wasn't angry if Maisie kicked over the milk or a rabbit scratched her. For one thing, she never considered the possibilities of the animals' being useful. They were simply companions, like people. I don't think it was out of sentimentality that I observed that they trusted her slightly more than the rest of us. After all, she never kicked them or cursed them and was impatient with us when we did.

But even Jane had trouble with the chickens. Like all our other animals, they were secondhand, the castoffs of the more experienced. Not realizing that we were buying a flock of hens past their prime, along with a nasty rooster, we unloaded our new experiment into their mite-ridden pen and waited for the eggs to come rolling in. And for about a month they did. We even marketed some. Then cold weather began to set in and the flow of eggs gradually diminished and finally stopped altogether.

Despite the elegant little societies of Hawthorne's and Hardy's fowl yards, I believe chickens invite indignities. Their exaggerated fright at the most innocent movement or noise belied their confident strutting and scratching. Their squawking and shoving over food was much more offensive than the mute greed of the rabbits and goats. In short, they were ridiculous creatures, puffed up and pompous over an insubstantial self-importance. Never did they try to escape, except as an unorganized group if the gate was left open. Above all they were stupid.

When we finally discovered, after pouring over our agricultural manuals, that they must be vermin-infested, we took action, trapping them in the hen house and then one by one catching them in a flurry of feathers and squawks and incontinent droppings, stuffing them in a sack of sulphur dust, and giving them a sound shaking.

Late in the winter they suffered a more serious setback. Roving dogs broke into the pen while we were gone for the day and decimated their numbers. As we drove up in the twilight, we saw the dogs slinking off in the brush along the irrigation ditch, white feathers drooping from their guilty muzzles. Chickens littered the field around the pen, some still struggling against death. The survivors huddled in a traumatized pile in a corner of the hen house. I had never seen even rabbits so frightened. Rabbits would at least fight back. But the chickens were immobilized.

It was a miserable cleanup job. No one had been fond of the chickens, yet watching them suffer in this hopeless way was somehow different from shaking them in sulphur dust. We kept the half that remained, partly as a memorial to their martyred relatives, partly because we didn't know what else to do with them.

The rooster had survived the massacre, which did not add to our respect for him. We must have had some romantic notion of his defending his harem even to the death. He was not safe to turn your back on, had to be approached gingerly, was insanely jealous of the territory of the chicken pen. It was best to edge around the fence, dart quickly into the house, dip out the feed, and hope to distract him into eating while you tipped water into the troughs. Once he began to do his battle dance, there was nothing to do but grab a broomstick and hope to fend him off till you could get out the gate.

Bees were the only other animals we kept for any length of time, and they were hardly in the animal class. For one thing they were totally independent of us. We neither fed nor watered them. The most caretaking we ever did on their behalf was to provide them with hives. Yet had they found themselves cramped for space they would have simply taken up quarters elsewhere, a move we lived in perpetual fear of once the spring came. The time we spent scraping wax from frames, inspecting for queen cells and disease, extracting honey from the frames, was only for our own benefit and in no way contributed to the bees' wellbeing. If anything, it was only a nuisance to them. In other words, we were completely the parasites in this situation, and if the arrangement turned out to be profitable in a small way, it was only because we had finally bought into a solvent corporation, one that had its collective head together, through no contribution of ours.

We got our eleven hives of bees in the winter, perfect timing for once since bees are conveniently indoors during cold weather. We had to be up all night, loading and unloading them, because they can't see in the dark and very few will venture out. In all, the hives required about forty hours of maintenance that spring, and then the honey flow began. Unlike Maisie, they didn't have to be nudged into reluctant production. They did not constantly try to escape like the rabbits. They did not make stupid noises or go into witless hysteria like the chickens. If they were inclined to be somewhat cranky on cloudy, windy days, at least their emotionalism was not without cause.

The bees above all inspired respect. Hence the suit of armor one was obliged to put on before approaching them. One slip of the scraping knife, one dead bee, and you could count on being covered by a battalion of enraged black Italians, all ready to give their unreflective lives for the protection of the hive. Jack eventually reached the point at which he could work with them uncovered, but cautiously. My own reaction to a bee attack, especially bees caught in my hair, was panic. There is something about the determination of a bee — relentlessly inhuman as only insects can be — that froze me with fear.

Still, it was that very inhumanness, that efficiency, that

perfect programming that demanded our respect. If we had turned the other animals out to go free, they could not have survived in an unprotected, unsubsidized environment for long. But the bees would not have missed our ministrations in the slightest. Yet they were by far the most productive for us, actually turning a small profit. The other animals we were forced to dispose of in one unsatisfactory way or another, but when we turned back to look at the farm for the last time, the beehives were still standing, humming in unattended activity. In no way did they ever reflect anything about us; there was some inexplicable barrier there that prevented any true intercourse between us.

All our animals but our bees were our captives. But there was one pair we at least caught in a fair chase. That was the two Welsh ponies that wandered over the rocky plain to the north of us. Wilson, our absentee landlord, had vaguely mentioned some ponies that had been included in the purchase of this land. Therefore, we had staked these two out as our legal, if unsuspecting, property.

It was late fall when we decided to round up the ponies, bring them into the corral, and train them to pull a plow for the spring planting. By this time Jerry was with us. He had had some years of experience as a cowboy on a large ranch in southern New Mexico and was fired up to bring these fat, vacationing animals into useful servitude for us. He persuaded the rest of us to buy some used collars and tack which he spent the evenings mending while telling tales around the fire of his cowboy days. He was a good storyteller; we hoped he was a great pony-breaker.

We woke one cold, windy morning to Jerry's insistence that this was the day for horsecatching. He had been watching their movements carefully, and today they were down in a field not far from the house. So about four of us put on our coats, wrapped up our heads, and trailed off behind Jerry to surround the ponies.

It was not nearly as easy as Jerry had led us to believe.

The field the horses were in had been plowed, and it made running, for us anyway, difficult. The gates of all the fields were down and the ponies had no trouble at all keeping a jump ahead of us. The wind whipped the raw dirt in our faces as we stumbled along, sometimes falling full length between the furrows.

After I got used to the situation's being hopeless, the chase became the most fun I had had since childhood. Indeed that's what it was like, running, whooping, and flailing our arms in the wind, trying to frighten the ponies into the ambush Jerry had prepared for them. We were soon breathless and panting from running, falling, and laughing. Still we ran, following Jerry's shouts of instructions to bar the gate, get them in the corner, not let them through. Up the bare hills and down into the steep arroyos where junipers and cottonwoods provided cover. Now and then catching sight of a spotted side as it dashed to safety again.

The chase went on for hours and seemed to have no point anymore — just the running, the wind, the falling, the laughing — when Jerry suddenly shouted to us from the bottom of a rocky slope. He had them cornered against the angle of a fence down by the river. We rushed and slid down the rocky hill, serious again about our purpose.

While we kept the ponies from escaping, Jerry hurriedly roped off a makeshift corral to keep them penned in. The ponies meanwhile snorted and stamped at the far end of the fence, sending up sprays of river water as they danced impatiently.

Jerry slipped into the enclosure with them and began talking to them low and beguilingly. They weren't having any of it and pranced away, insulted.

It was like a dream by now. A long, drawn-out, slow-motion dream dance. Jerry advancing, horses retreating. Around and around. We were in a strange, beautiful world, the wind and the water whirling around us, the light falling into the arroyo illuminating a dream of chase, battle, entreaty. I wished it could have gone on forever. The wild, rolling eyes of the ponies watched Jerry crooning to them. At last he slipped a rope halter around the neck of one and then the other. Once the rope was on, they stood surprisingly docile. It was afternoon when we led them, plodding and balky, back up the rocks, over the fields, and into the corral.

For a week Jerry worked with the ponies, leading them round and round the corral. It would be a long time, he admitted, before he could get them to work together in harness.

As it turned out, he never had the opportunity to try. One afternoon Sally started out the kitchen door only to discover Suarez, our nearest neighbor, leading the two ponies by their ropes out of the corral and across the road toward his own pasture. "Jerry," she called, "Jack. Come quick. Something's wrong."

Something was indeed wrong from Suarez's point of view. When Jerry and Jack accosted him in the road, he was ready with a tongue-lashing of which only a few words were in English, but enough of them for us to get the general drift of his sentiments. The ponies, he claimed, were his. They never had been Wilson's. If Wilson had any ponies of his own, let him produce them. And furthermore, we were not to impose on his hospitality any further. He had no truck with horse thieves. He had been looking for these ponies for a week now and had even alerted the sheriff to their disappearance. We were lucky we weren't all in jail.

Although the circumstances of their departure were unpleasant, I was almost relieved to see the ponies go. They ate tremendous quantities of hay, and Jerry had told us that when we started working them they would have to get grain. Besides, I never really believed the two stubborn beasts could be trained to the plow. We had already had the best part of them — the chase.

Taken all together, the animals gave me something deeper and more pervasive than "learning." They became a strata, a vein, in what was me. My worldview, my *blik,* as the philosopher R. M. Hare would say, now has in it the darting rabbit eyes staring at me with no recognition or trust from a hollow in the hay. The weak, watery eyes of Furball I discount; he did not truly trust us, but had simply given up his rabbit spirit through some congenital defect, and though we pitied him (and thus did not eat him), our caretaking was only a token of our guilt.

For this paradox of guilt and necessity weighed down upon us every time Jack laid the lead pipe to the cortex of a palpitating rabbit body and nailed its hind legs to the shed wall to skin it. Thoreau went to the woods to live life close to the bone and suck its marrow. Christ starved in the wilderness to be tempted. But we found ourselves shivering at the sight of the bloody reality that confronted us on the shed wall. It's easy enough to be an optimistic pantheist when one is growing beans. But when you are imprisoning and killing an animal whose heart beats faster than your own, without even a fair chase, when you have to beat the innocent dogs away from the blood coagulating in the sand, when you know that given even four days without food you would be willing to eat the dogs themselves, and in forty days one another, you begin to touch the uneven outer limits of your possibilities.

I have eaten *cabrito* on a holiday in Mexico and know the delicious, crusty, sweet taste of the kid's milkfed flesh. I could sink my carnivore's teeth into it tomorrow with relish. But when one stands watching two ivory-colored kids butting one another in play and weighs whether this sight is more important than the sweet taste of their flesh, the ominous question of how we got this way begins to form on the horizon of the mind, no bigger than a man's hand.

And once we begin we are well into it. So you are suddenly swamped with vegetarian guilt while your hutch is full of rabbits. Do you expiate your own guilt by loosing them to their natural predators? Do you at the least demand that they stop breeding? Do you clearheadedly assess the life-style of aboriginal hunters and gatherers who take their "fair" place in the quest for food? Usually you hustle them off for someone else to worry over or you live with your guilt and meat.

However, becoming a vegetarian does not resolve the dilemma. Chickens, eggs; goats, milk. And the finer points of the law. The rabbits could smell the original sin on us. And if the goats knew which side their bread was buttered on, they also knew enough not to be grateful. If the chickens were hysterical, was it not with stir-craziness? Yet how do we live without premeditated exploitation? Unless we live as saints, facing early extermination, or as animals? There seems no simply human way to live, except in the dark crack between guilt and necessity.

Perhaps in this we are closer to the insects than we admit. The ants who keep herds of aphids. Larvae feeding on the living body of their host. We have a horror and a fascination for the bee's efficiency. They do not stop at hounding useless males from the pack; they dispatch them at the door. There are no disobedient bees, no social deviants. Even their dancing is not, like the kids', from sheer exuberance of wellbeing or for fun, but to locate for the community new nectar fields.

But in the end we sneer at the hive society. We secretly cheer (while cursing) the ones who know we are not to be trusted, who acquiesce to no coexistence treaty with us, who never give up their attempts at escape. If we were an exploited animal, that is how we would hope to behave, and not like the poor stupid, addled chickens or the exhausted Furball. Whenever I heard that defiant thump of a rabbit's hind leg, something in my dark insides laughed exultantly: Don't give up, my little enemy. Your senses tell you right — I'm trying to kill you. Resist, resist your death, resist me. For as long as you resist, I know you are real. The world is real and not just a reflection of myself. And whatever it is in me that makes it necessary for me to kill you is being resisted and has not yet swallowed the whole, real world.

4

> To the woman he said, "I shall greatly increase your pain and your pregnancy. In pain you shall bear children and yet you shall long for your husband. And he shall dominate you."
> — Genesis 3:16

> Men have died and worms have eaten them, but not for love.
> — Shakespeare, *Romeo and Juliet*

Packed in among the dishes, the furniture, and the tools we brought with us to New Mexico were certain old patterns we had hoped to leave behind, and were in fact sure we had, until we began to try to live our new life. Then we discovered, rumpled but familiar, the same stale attitudes and ways of seeing one another we thought we had abandoned with our jobs, schools, and American society.

The first of these to come to light was the tension between the men and women. Seen through the eyes of the great modern fantasy, of course, there was nothing ambiguous about what we were doing: we were simply out for as much uninterrupted, indiscriminate, licentious sexuality as we could get. Undoubtedly those sorts of desires are possible in a solitary individual. They are even possible in a group for a short space of time — say, one evening. But when a collection of people, all with very different backgrounds, expectations, and ways of being pleased, come together to live for an extended period, that fantasy deflates from a hundred different pressures. Not that that fantasy was one that any of us had seriously entertained. The imagined worlds of Fellini were never anything but repugnant to us. What we desired was innocence, not debauchery.

Naturally, our attempts at defining and regaining the innocence we craved were sad little scenarios, but illumined now and again by some small hint of rightness that kept us struggling, never very successfully, after our obscure vision. Two or three, sunning naked on the rocks like soft, vulnerable lizards, could feel like contented children. But the discovery that what we had thought was our well-protected outdoor shower was being lecherously observed by our neighbors filled us with bitter indignation.

Everyone craved an innocent sexuality, but nowhere could we find a pattern for it. Animals were no very happy model. Cats yowling in desperation; strange dogs invading our house when one of ours was in heat; the ferocious couplings of our rabbits when, as often as not, either the buck or the doe would be torn and bleeding after the encounter; the strutting cock in the chicken yard; the smelly billy we took our Maisie to for "servicing"; the dead drones strewn outside the hives after the pleasureless attacks of the workers — none of these appealed to us, although we could see their reflections in our own relationships. We did not despise the necessity that seemed to drive the animals we lived with; we only knew that human sexuality must mean something more.

Not that there wasn't a certain amount of prowling instinct that inhabited some of our hearts. The unattached people particularly felt their lot to be more than a little hard, having come from centers of population where there were plenty of other young people also sniffing about for someone, to a barren New Mexico farm thirty-five miles from the nearest town. No wonder that as the summer ripened there was more and more hitchhiking to Santa Fe for the weekend.

But for those who came with some relationship already formed or who developed one afterwards, matters were little better. In fact, in this stark setting, problems seemed to be magnified to almost unbearable proportions. For example, Don and Janet had been living together for at least a year before we came to New Mexico. Previously they had lived in a campus commune, pursuing a life of what newsmagazines commonly call radical activism — the Food Conspiracy, women's liberation, the peace movement, free schools. Yet their relationship had all the dreary clichés of any middle-class marriage.

Janet was a tall, full-blown blonde, with the face and abundant hair of a Renaissance Venus. Protective and motherly, she was one of the few women who took enough interest in the two children to read to them, sew for them, or teach them anything new. Yet she was just as protective and motherly towards Don. Every morning she would get up and fix his breakfast separately from everyone else's because he liked to sleep late and didn't take well to boiled wheat or oatmeal. When people began to protest, she defended this as Don's peculiar eccentricity that was a mark of his personal freedom.

"Can't you even see what you're doing?" Sally would scream at her. "For all your big ideas about being liberated, you're nothing more than a slave to Don's every whim."

Don himself came from a wealthy suburban family with a caricature cutthroat businessman for a father. He never tired of telling the story of how his father had made him a standing offer of $1000 to cut his hair, which he had heroically turned down. As time wore on and the story thin, we all began to wish Don had been a little less principled and a lot more practical. Almost the sole content of Don's work was the rebuilding of his Harley Davidson motorcycle which had broken down right after getting him and Janet to New Mexico. He had a real aversion to animals and gardening and threatened, like a petulant child, not to take his turn at dishwashing if people weren't more respectful of his freedom. Yet as long as his demands were gratified, he was good natured and agreeable.

His dark handsomeness was a perfect foil to Janet's

fairness. But their dependencies fitted together in a much more sinister way. Don was essentially Janet's child. She protected him from our attacks, coddled him, acceded to his wishes, was at the bottom of her heart afraid of losing him. He laughed at her nagging the way a confident, spoiled child will laugh at its mother, but deepened his dependence on her daily. Sexually, they were incestuous.

It was not pleasant for the rest of us to watch this being acted out. First, it was all too typical of the homes some of us had come out of. The demanding father, the acquiescing mother, the nagging, the cruelty, the fear of losing love. We already knew that what we wanted was something different from this. Yet it had followed us like an unlaid ghost in the form of two people who intellectually knew better, who had read all the right books and belonged to the right groups but were powerless to change their behavior.

Moreover, there was a great gulf between Janet and the other women, who saw her as their betrayer. She was not playing fair; she was only managing to hold Don by satisfying his childish whims, and since several of them found Don remarkably attractive, they thought this rigged the competition. The others were simply enraged at the sight of a woman, a sister, prostrating herself so servilely and thus disgracing their sex.

On the other hand, Don had only superficial friendships with the men, since his childishness was resented or envied or both. They felt towards him as the older children feel towards the baby of a family who is granted privileges they never had. Thus both Don and Janet were isolated from other friendships in the groups and forced to rely all the more on each other exclusively, wearing the ruts of their relationship ever deeper.

Wayne and Faye had known one another only a few weeks before coming to New Mexico. Yet Wayne had quickly conceived one of those dark, brooding passions for Faye, who, unfortunately for him, did not reciprocate. At first she had found it convenient enough to have a handy partner, someone to talk and joke and sleep with. But soon she began feeling crowded, especially when Wayne suggested that they fix up one of the outbuildings for just the two of them. She was not all *that* committed, was not prepared to cut off whatever other possibilities might arise. She was out to seek her fortune, and Wayne, though fun enough in his own way, was no treasure.

Wayne was overwhelmed at this news. To his eyes Faye encompassed every quality he could ever wish for in a woman, and to be denied his heart's desire at this early stage made life a bleak prospect indeed. He proceeded with his plans to fix up one of the buildings and moved in alone. Faye suffered only minor twinges of guilt at disappointing him, but he withdrew from the rest of human society to grieve with a vengeance. Of course, he never really gave up and continued to entreat Faye to join him, and she continued to refuse, at first gently and later with annoyance.

The women treated Wayne's morose lovesickness with ridicule for the most part. For one thing it was morally wrong to try to force Faye into an arrangement against her obvious will. Wayne was not a gentleman. The men, although they didn't really much care one way or another, still felt a trifle uneasy about the situation and were not quite so inclined to laugh at Wayne's sulks. Whether out of a fearful secret knowledge through which they could see themselves in his position or just a greater respect for Wayne's feelings, they would frown at the women's giggling at his departing back as he disappeared after each meal back down the path to his hovel, his hands jammed into his jeans pockets and his head down.

Faye continued to be discreet but indiscriminate, keeping one eye on Don and one on every new male visitor. She played her flute in the summer evenings, was careful to achieve just the right kind of clever antiqueness with her clothes, tried seriously but unsuccessfully to accept her share of the work and responsibility, was generous with her resources. But everyone was made uneasy by her restlessness, her prowling search for a man, the feeling that, given half a chance, she would desert. And although her friendships with other women were more solid than Janet's, still they didn't trust her, especially to respect any of their established relationships with men.

Eventually Faye did find someone, at least temporarily. In the next village, where we got our mail, lived two brothers, rather raunchy types who had accrued enough money working in the Detroit car mills to buy their own land. Their parents were Russian immigrants and their life had been hard, unsoftened by even those meager consolations the middle class offers its children. They were strong, hard workers whenever they were not drunk or high, and usually good natured when they were, although something dangerous lurked there too. Joe, the younger brother, had been on heroin for a while and still played around with it from time to time.

Our community was friendly with them, but hesitant to be too neighborly, the usual reaction of protected radical theoreticians when they confront the raw unmanageable material of their theories.

Faye, however, for whatever glamorous allure such a strange background held, had at last found someone with a recklessness to match her own. His idea of a good time was walking as close to the edge of disaster as possible, which suited Faye's own propensities for pushing life to the extremes. So when Joe's brother went back to Michigan in the fall to make another bundle on the assembly line, Faye moved in with Joe.

They lived in an old one room adobe shack on his property. It was a cold, damp autumn. We still saw Faye occasionally, of course. And while several of us were yet a little huffy about her having left us, we were also relieved at not having to worry about *when* she would do it anymore.

Faye did not fare so well, however. For the first couple of weeks she was romantically enthusiastic about the arrangement. She ordered the tiny house to her satisfaction, helped haul water from the village well, learned the peculiarities of the wood stove. Then the clashes began. While she had found Joe's rough offhandedness immensely satisfying to her sexual prototype of masculinity, when that same attitude got up out of the bed — or rather demanded that she get up out of the bed and fix his breakfast — or even when it demanded her attendance in bed when she didn't feel like it, the picture began to pale. She had always been a fierce liberationist, valuing as she did her own freedom. But Joe, who had known only a much mistreated mother and sisters who had been taken advantage of at an early age, hadn't the least inkling of Faye's desires for respect and independence and didn't much care to learn. His life had always been catch-as-catch-can and devil-take-the-hindmost, and since he had survived so far, no mean task, he saw no reason to change for some softheaded woman.

Faye learned what it was to evade the raucous demands not only of Joe, but of the drunk buddies he brought home as well. And by the time she found herself being knocked around for not obeying, the glamour had worn as thin as her patience. She packed up her belongings, paid us a farewell visit, and hitched further west, still looking for that Eldorado that contained both the Marlboro Man and Henry David Thoreau.

Unrequited love was as abundant in our midst as it is in folk songs. First there was Faye and Wayne, then later Lillian and Jerry. Lillian joined us in New Mexico immediately after she had obtained a very unsatisfactory divorce. Not that there were any children involved or even any complicated property settlement. In fact, it was not contested in any way. Her husband, an anthropologist, had simply left her after six years of marriage without a word of explanation. The unresolved rejection rankled in Lillian's neat, tidy soul. She decided to redo herself entirely. She cut off her hair, bought new clothes, quit her high-salaried job, and set out to seek her fortune. Her first stop was with us. She arrived on the train with the four white rabbits, ready to set up an efficient, productive rabbit ranch. But even Lillian's bustling efficiency broke down before the massive, amorphous unwieldiness of destiny in the desert. Yet, much that did get done was owing to her. She repaired rabbit hutches, saw to their care, made herself a private room in the attic that no one had bothered with, canned tomatoes, and dried apples.

Jerry didn't join us till the fall. He came out of much the same sort of rough and ready background as Joe, but being a voracious reader, had been cross-pollinated with the ideas in the air about new lifestyles. Being extremely clever at making things, he was much more interested in the pragmatics of such ideas — developing a methane power plant, a wind generator, solar heated buildings — than in new human relationships. In fact, he joined us right after having been released from the state hospital where he had been incarcerated for beating up his mother.

A tall, lanky cowboy, he was as strong and willing as they come, painfully eager for a human company that would accept him and appreciate his worth. He was also a great storyteller, having that kind of checkered past that makes for endless tales. He was immediately a great favorite of everyone.

It didn't take him long to single out Lillian as his favorite. She had grit, determination, resourcefulness — all characteristics he valued highly. And besides, she was small and pretty, even dainty, which intrigued him. But Lillian was having none of it. Although she felt a brotherly affection for Jerry, he was not at all her sort. She made none of the mistakes of impetuosity that Faye had made, yet the situation was no better. Jerry was as hopelessly infatuated as Wayne had been.

When he came he had been quite honest with us about his background. He had even showed us the antidepressant medication that had been prescribed for him in the hospital. But he had proved himself to be so easygoing and agreeable that we had finally chalked it all up to another great blunder by the forces of Society. After his suit to Lillian began to be clearly rejected (that took a while to make clear), he began a tailspin into the outer reaches of depression. At first he was only gloomy and uncommunicative. When this had no effect on Lillian, he withdrew even deeper into his own special darkness. He would no longer go outdoors and work, then he wouldn't even leave his room, and finally he took to his bed.

The rest of us were simply bewildered by this behavior. Lillian of course refused to give in or to offer any false hope. She was just as offended by this undisguised emotional blackmail as Faye had been. Our genteel backgrounds had not prepared us to cope with this almost Sicilian solicitation. It was such utterly bad form, especially to the women, to push oneself forward where one was so obviously not wanted.

Yet we couldn't simply shrug and smile wryly at Jerry the way we had with Wayne. Wayne had isolated himself and been dreadfully touchy and tender and eventually had packed up his broken heart and left, but Jerry was a more drastic case. The deeper his depression grew, the more dangerous he became. He refused to take his medication as we urged him. If he was going to suffer, so were we all. And it was obvious he was spoiling for a fight, someone to vent his frustrated feelings on.

One winter morning, without a word to anyone, he began packing all his belongings, making a great clatter and fuss so that we all got the message that he intended to leave. Lillian was elated and joked nervously in the kitchen with Sally about her large, lumbering Lothario who was finally giving up. Everyone had learned not to ask Jerry any questions since they got either no answer or very unsatisfactory ones, but they watched his packing furtively.

When I saw him stalk off to the bathhouse to retrieve his things from there, I felt a sudden pang of remorse.

Perhaps we hadn't done all we might to make things easier for Jerry. With his crumpled cowboy hat and torn jacket he looked destitute of all human friendship. I could approach him more easily than anyone else; my matron's status seemed to hold some special significance for him. I followed him down to the bathhouse, determined to talk.

It was a grey, dreary day. Inside the dank building musty hay and cornstalks were piled in the corner, harboring mice and spiders. We sat on the side of the bathtub to talk and propped our feet on the blackened wood stove we heated the bath water on.

I began in my gentlest voice, hoping to gain entry to Jerry's hearing by appealing to whatever his idea of feminine was, yet not sure what tone I might unwittingly take that would rouse his wrath against women and what he had suffered at their hands. I never knew at what moment I might tread on some territory mined with terrible memories and associations.

"Are you leaving, Jerry?"

A long pause. "Yep."

"Why? We don't want you to." Not exactly true but it *could* have been true under other conditions.

"She does."

"You mean Lillian?"

He ignored my stupid question and reflected on his own assertion. "She'll be happier when I'm not around. It's either her or me. I can't stand it any longer."

"But you're both important to us, Jerry. We need you as much as her." True enough, but a not quite fair way of putting it. And totally ignoring the fact that Lillian would never leave on Jerry's account.

"That may be, but I've got to get out of here. I thought when I came here that this was really heaven, that I'd found what I'd been looking for all my life. But I got fooled again, and I've got to move on. I appreciate what you and Jack and everyone has done for me, but it's just not working out."

"But Lillian's not the only fish in the pond," I protested. "You can't let something like this spoil all your plans." The look on his face warned me not to push this any further. I hadn't taken his pain seriously enough.

"Well," he said gruffly, standing up to leave, "I know when I've got to leave. Thanks for everything."

"Goodbye, Jerry. There'll be a place for you whenever you want to come back." I stood up and gave him a farewell peck on the cheek. Perhaps he felt a small bit better that someone had broken through his own stubborn silence and at least said goodbye properly. But it was no more than a bandaid on a festering wound. There was no healing and no desire for healing. Jerry's disease had become his identity. He climbed in the back of the truck Jack had waiting at the gate. He sat on the side, balancing his duffle bag between his knees and not looking back.

Sally had joined us in New Mexico carefree and unattached. She was one of those rare eager-hearted people ready to love almost anyone on a moment's notice. When her art teacher had assigned her the project of designing chairs for a restaurant so uncomfortable that no one would linger more than thirty minutes, she had dropped out of art school in a moral huff. Now she had ambitions of becoming a weaver, if she could ever find some place to set up a loom. The first summer she spent shuttling back and forth between Moriah and Santa Fe, trying to find a job, trying to find a spot, trying to find what she called an "ogle man." She was small and svelte, full of high spirits and daring, and was almost everyone's darling, especially to the children, among whom she really counted herself. She could make up funny songs and games on long afternoons, put together elaborate costumes for them, and generally make our hard times appear a lark.

But the more Sally brightened, the more shadows seemed to hedge her in. Her family history had some rather large dark spots. And the friends that she made so easily and gave herself to so freely were not always as loyal and loving as she.

As fall came on and the handful of short-lived jobs she had held during the tourist season in Santa Fe dried up, she came back to the farm to settle in for the winter. Meanwhile we had added another new member, Simon, a silversmith and college drop-out. In contrast to Sally, Simon was solemn, slow, and liked to meditate a lot. Once in a while a ripple of humor or anger would cross the otherwise placid surface of his psyche, but mostly he worked at being as inscrutable as a Buddha.

None of us could ever understand what drew the two of them together to begin with. True, almost anyone was instantly attracted to Sally, but then she was much more vivacious and open than Simon seemed to think necessary for the properly spiritual life. On the other hand, skinny Simon with only his golden wavy hair, of which he was secretly vain, to recommend him physically, did not at all seem the sort Sally would take as a lover. He was no "ogle man" to be sure and scorned levity. There were times though when I think he was hungry for it and longed to join in, only he didn't know how and was afraid of looking ridiculous. So we stood by and watched the liaison develop, not wanting to put our oar in where it wasn't wanted, but expecting no good to come from it. And of course we weren't disappointed.

They soon decided to move into the same outbuilding that the ill-fated Wayne had fixed up for Faye. The farmhouse was depressing enough, but this was even worse. Directly below the irrigation canal, it was always damp and moldy. There being only one small window, and that one facing north, it was also dark. The floor was dirt, but Wayne had plastered the walls inside, which at least slowed the crumbling process. There was, of course, no water or heat. These inauspicious surroundings as winter began to set in would have put a strain on all but the hardiest of alliances. Needless to say, nothing Simon undertook was ever hardy, but rather, speculative.

Soon Sally grew unnaturally morose. At first she was reluctant to talk about her situation, feeling it would be disloyal to talk about Simon behind his back. But finally she admitted to Lillian and me that she was utterly miserable. Simon wanted affection with half his heart, but pushed it away with the other half. Touching and kissing and laughing were painful to him. He wanted Sally to be more serious, meaning more respectful of his self-consciously ascetic ways. Still she felt there were enough good things buried in Simon so as not to want to give the relationship up. Yet she was freezing to death inside and out.

They never fought, of course. Pacifistic Simon would have died rather than openly shouted at someone. It was silence, silence and cold and pretense that stifled them. He wanted affection and warmth but was ashamed of wanting it and consequently told himself, and Sally, that it was superior not to want it. And Sally, having made a commitment to Simon out of who knows what sort of desperation, hung on, refusing to admit the defeat of her desire to love and be loved by someone. Yet she weakened every day and grew more tearful.

Mercifully, it ended at last with her illness. She had to have an operation in a large city hospital, and this took her away for a month. Simon, of course, never gave a sign that her going altered anything in his life. He was solicitous in a distant way about her health. But if there was any hole left in his life by her absence, he never let anyone know.

When she came back, she and Simon did not take up their old relationship. They were stiffly friendly but that was all. Whatever other resolution they reached between them we never knew. Sally's desperate search continued, and Simon grew more confirmed in his detachment.

Not long after this, Sally, Lillian, and I were staying at a friend's apartment in town recuperating from a newly diagnosed case of paratyphoid. We were enjoying the easy warmth of the furnace heat, the relatively clean surroundings, a flush toilet, and hot water without having to feel apologetic to the others back at the farm. In this cozy atmosphere we waxed philosophical about relationships between men and women, a subject that often preoccupied us.

"I don't think that I will ever again have a permanent relationship with any man," Lillian said. "It's too much hassle for too little reward."

"But I can't live without men," protested Sally. "It's no fun."

"Well," said Lillian in her most no-nonsense tone, "that doesn't have to mean anything permanent. Why do we have to hurt and hurt just for someone to sleep with and a chuck under the chin once in a while? From now on for me it's only going to be transient affairs." She savored the last two words as only a resolute apostate from respectability can.

"Transient affairs," Sally agreed. And at the time it truly seemed like the most sensible solution in the world, a way of cutting your losses and at least not decreasing the rewards. And though at the time it seemed so satisfactory, I know neither of them has strictly stuck to her plan.

These are all stories of people bound with no legal or familial ties, people trying on and discarding with some facsimile of freedom various sorts of relationships. But what of Jack and I who had been married ten years and had two daughters?

Our marriage had become a painful, comfortable trap, padded with plastic apartments, several degrees, teaching positions, and Bankamericards. Somehow those youthful pictures we had carried around inside us for years, plans of what we were going to do with our precious lives, were aborting, dying without ever having seen the light of day. We had been to Europe and Mexico, bought a camper, and spent nights on the Gulf Coast beach, a vacation in the Rockies, and a summer in Taos. But these were only sops for the excitement we longed for.

On one particular day distinct in my memory, all four of us were sitting around our dinner table, watching the heat turn the asphalt to black bubbles and the newly planted tree outside our apartment window drooping in the blasting sun, when the despairing thought flashed through my brain that life would never be any different than this, that we were caught. There was no way out.

My notion of the trap at that time was primarily economic. We couldn't afford just to give up our jobs and explore the world. We had two children to support. It was not until these dissatisfactions became irrational resentments against one another and each began to see the other as a part of his own trap that we were forced to find a way out. Even an animal, if it is desperate enough, will gnaw off its own leg to escape the trap. And in such a desperate state we went about gnawing at one another.

Not that our goals were at variance, although they were rather amorphous and vague. We both wanted something we called freedom: freedom from the kinds of time limitations ordinary jobs demanded, freedom from meaningless conventions and conformity, freedom from an "unnatural," hemmed-in life. But most of all, freedom from emptiness.

I remember the long, empty, bored Sunday afternoons straight out of *The Wasteland*. "What shall we do, what shall we ever do?" Go see equally bored friends, get up a party, drive out into the country. The Sunday paper scattered around the living room, the girls cross and fidgety, a dull, cottony taste in the mouth. We grew as quarrelsome as children shut up indoors on a perpetual rainy day. Yet there were still moments when we shared our gropings after something more, the ineffable "more," more than this dead-end, pointless life. And these moments kept us knit together, however tenuously.

We tried separate households for a year. We were 250 miles apart, but one or the other of us commuted almost every weekend. As the experiment developed, however, I was even less satisfied than ever. I had the children and a fulltime job. Although I had said this was what I wanted, a chance to earn my own living, be on my own two feet, I was dreadfully lonely. I had gnawed off my leg and escaped from the trap, but found myself ambiguously free and definitely crippled.

Jack, meanwhile, had found an exciting new role to play at. Having been married since our freshman year in college, he had never known anything but the constant economic imperative of provide, provide. Now he was able to loosen up, grow grungy, get inflamed with radical politics. He had a bachelor apartment with a friend and lived the free and easy life of a graduate student.

It was during this year that we formulated our plans for New Mexico. We had wiggled loose enough from the structures that bound us to begin to see a way out. I was ready to move on, and Jack, although his life was more appealing than it had been, was nonetheless becoming increasingly alienated from competitive academic degree-gathering. His participation in the campus strike that spring was the death blow to his teaching aspirations.

Our need for one another was compulsive. After ten years of changes, each had become a repository of the history of the other. No one else in the whole world knew us so well as we knew each other. We relied on one another to know who we were; if we were cut off from one another, we would also be cut off from our own identities, our own selves. But at the same time, we hated one another for this dependence. It is not always pleasant to be reminded of who you are, accused of your identity. There were times when we wanted to smash the mirror staring us in the face.

Jack, for instance, was such a conflicting bundle of impulses that it was almost impossible for him to act except out of frustration with those conflicts. No one's soul ever burned with a whiter flame against social injustices than Jack's. He could have made a great crusader or guerrilla, and perhaps would have had he not been encumbered by a family. Yet at the same time, he had grown up in a lower middle-class home and had built into him all those aspirations for comfort, for easy movement, for conspicuous signs of success. To walk into a bank now and be hassled because his clothes and hair were not respectable filled him with both indignation and shame. And the frustration of not being able to reconcile these two conflicting emotions often exploded into irrational anger.

He demanded a very high standard of conduct from the other people at Moriah — loyalty, hard work, unselfishness, order — nothing more than he expected from himself. But when these expectations were coupled with the prevailing tenet of counterculture faith, namely, that it is wrong to make demands on anyone, that personal freedom is the highest good, the combustion caused by the friction between the two ideas brought down fire on everyone's heads.

Jack in a rage was terrible to behold, a cross between Jeremiah and Rasputin. His nuclear family had borne the brunt of his frustrations with the futility of academia and his clinging to its security. Now his extended family was catching it because we all had an ideological illusion of freedom while needing a strict discipline to survive at Moriah. Not having the ironclad personality to withstand his thunderous assaults, the weaker ones were scared away by the end of the first summer.

My own unconfessed intention in gathering other people about us was to dilute the intensity of our private partnership. I wanted to form an alliance against Jack, to throw up a barricade of unsuspecting bodies between ourselves. Other people, I was convinced, would sympathize and take my part against this tyrant. Eventually there would be others who knew me as well as Jack did and who, of course, would love me. Then I would be free! I wouldn't need Jack anymore. He, I thought with secret vengeance, could go choke on his own anger and disappointments. For my part, I would have built up a backlog of friends who recognized my worth. I would never need to be lonely again.

Our motives, then, were the darkest and most devious of all, sometimes hidden even from ourselves. While everyone else's purposes were not always in line with the revolutionary rhetoric they espoused, at least they were usually quite transparent. But in our private battle, all others were merely weapons we used against each other.

Of course, we were not quite so skilled at manipulation as we had supposed. Life resisted us too firmly. Our extended family, each person with his or her own personal goals, outmaneuvered us continually. And in the end, instead of the lines being drawn between my side and Jack's, we found ourselves back on the same side of the barricades, we against them.

This in itself was unhealthy. We were not really able to take seriously other people's needs. Our first demand was that they sacrifice all their private dreams to ours — the success of the commune at Moriah. Then they could go on with their lives with their leftover time and energy. Every time someone left, we tried to appear understanding. But in our hearts we scorned them as failures. These desertions, as we saw them, did, however, accomplish the task of driving us up against the wall together. We learned, once and for all, the meaning of "forsaking all others."

This didn't put an end to our terrible fights, but at least more mutual territory was marked out in them now that there was no deluding ourselves with dreams of a diluted marriage. I remember one particularly hot, dusty day when after an explosive parting with one of our original group we quarreled over what seemed to me Jack's overly generous offers to stock the deserter up with food and take him the thirty miles down to the main highway where the chances of hitching were better.

"Gas costs money," I complained. "And he's freeloaded long enough. If he's so anxious to do his own thing, let it be his *own* thing."

Jack was suddenly furious, more enraged than I had seen him in months. The whole argument escalated beyond anything I had intended.

"You can't talk that way," he yelled, throwing his keys

across the room. He pushed me aside and stormed out the bedroom door, slamming it behind him. I followed, aghast at what was happening, sure that if ever we needed to stick together against the rest of the world it was now, when everyone else was deserting us. In the living room he was crying, great heaving sobs, and pounding his fists into the plaster. I was crying and beseeching him to tell me what was the matter.

"You," he screamed, "you and your stupid, grasping, tight-fistedness." He paused, and for a moment I held back all the justifications, all the instances of my overtaxed generosity. And that moment of restraint was a gift of grace, because instead of degenerating into the usual recriminations against one another's failures, it gave him the chance to say: "I don't care. I don't care if people take advantage of me or if I give away more than they 'deserve.' If I can't do that, if I can't, once in a while, be magnanimous, then I don't care about living this life. It doesn't mean anything if it's only fighting and grasping and holding off the rest of the world. If that's what life is, I don't want it, I don't want it."

I caught my breath as the words came out of his mouth. He was right, he was right. To always be cringing in a corner and afraid of advantages being taken, to be always in the protective position — even if we lost everything (and heaven knows we had little enough to lose then) — it wasn't worth even life itself. Whatever other secondary goals we had — a homestead of our own, a free life, whatever — there was something more essential to both of us than that, and without it we would die from a dream gone sour.

It was only the beginning of the clarity, of course. It was to be another while before we could formulate any better what was at the bottom of both of us that kept us together. But it was a true beginning, and it was fortunate that it happened then because, although we didn't know it, we were just entering a chapter of our story that would be more difficult and bitter than anything we had known before.

5

> Cursed is the ground because of you. In grief you shall eat of it all the days of your life. Thorns and thistles shall spring up for you and you shall eat the plants of the field. With the sweat of your face you shall eat bread until you return to the ground.
> — Genesis 3:17-19

> a flower within a flower whose history
> (within the mind) crouching
> among the ferny rocks, laughs at the names
> by which they think to trap it. Escapes! Never by
> running but by lying still
> — William Carlos Williams, *Paterson*

If there was a dark gulf filled with ancient enmity between us and the animals, there was an even deeper, more impenetrable mystery that infused the land. This was not the familiar, rich, domesticated farmland of the Midwest, leveled, parceled, and calculable. It was rugged open range where the few fences were built to keep stock out, not in.

According to old reports, the ground had been covered with range grasses that were belly-high on the horses of the Spanish settlers. Don Juan Oñate, entering for the first time what is now New Mexico, wrote to the Viceroy, the Count of Monterey, on March 2, 1659:

> It is a land abounding in flesh of buffalo, goats with hideous horns, and turkeys.... There are many wild and ferocious beasts, lions, bears, wolves, tigers, penicas, ferrets, porcupines, and other animals whose hides they tan and use. Towards the west there are bees and very white honey, of which I am sending a sample. Besides, there are vegetables, a great abundance of the best and

greatest salines in the world, and a very great many kinds of very rich ores, as I stated above.

Now only the thinnest tussocks of buffalo grass grew sparsely over the rocky bones of the earth. That and several varieties of cactus. A hundred years of overgrazing had left the land despoiled, stripped to the bone. Handfuls of Herefords still wandered over it, ripping up any green shoot from between the rocks. Herds of horses were turned loose on the open range to fare as best they could. Life on this land was hard, and the people could ill afford any suburban sentimentality about animals.

Still the earth retained its own strength, but it was a strength not friendly to human enterprise. It was a land aloof and ascetic. It had suffered much under the hand of humans, and its austerity was beautiful but unyielding. Early in the morning when the sun was catching whatever nighttime moisture had been left clinging to the thick grey gourd leaves, there was a hint of the softness and abundance the land had once known. Wasps climbed drunkenly down into the yucca bloom caverns. Bees hummed around the chamisa and cactus blossoms. Jack rabbits stuck up their long ears along the irrigation canal. Among the cottonwoods birds were calling. Walking out upon the world in its early morning joy, one caught the reflected light of fresh creation. The sun fell at a long gentle slope upon the waking world. But a few hours later it was beating straight down, pressing all life down into the hollows of shade.

It was only along the river or the canals that anything could grow. By the middle of the summer the river itself was low and sluggish as its waters were drained away to irrigate long, narrow alfalfa fields, cut narrower with each succeeding generation's inheritance.

Our neighbor, Mr. Suarez, an old bachelor, lived with his five fierce dogs that he fed a trough of biscuit dough every evening. He was considered the most successful farmer along the river valley. Besides his own fields, he leased all he could lay his hands on from the surrounding community and worked it with his new machinery from dawn to dark. He was neither Protestant nor Anglo, yet a sterner example of what is popularly called the Puritan work ethic never lived. Every moment of daylight was spent on his tractor, his mower, his baler. He raised acres of tomatoes and melons he could not possibly eat nor sell. He grew fruit trees that littered the ground with untouched pears and peaches. He dotted the fields with bale upon bale of alfalfa hay. In the winters he had pneumonia. And he did it all alone, an old man in his late sixties. At first he was cautiously friendly to us, but after the incident with the ponies, he grew suspicious and edgy. It must have done his old, bitter heart good to see the late-rising gringos hacking away at their little garden plot with pickaxes.

We finally picked a spot right below the irrigation canal for a garden. There was plenty of seepage further down the slope, so we expected this spot to be fairly cooperative with our efforts. We soon learned not to expect the ground to yield anything easily. It was rust red and tough as nails. The weeds that grew there had long adapted their slender root systems to the nearly impenetrable soil. We confidently bought a new eight-horsepower rotary tiller and set to work to break the back of that patch. Instead the tiller broke. We discovered that the only way to break up the soil was literally with pickaxes.

During the winter months we shovelled truck load after truck load of manure out of a rancher's horse pen and dumped it on the garden. We hauled loads of sludge from the nearest town's sewer plant. By the following spring we could turn it over with a shovel and use the tiller some.

Suarez was contemptuous of all our back-breaking efforts. His idea of farming this land was to wrassle it down, breaking it with a heavy plow. His furrows were yard-wide wounds, doused liberally with the strongest fertilizers he could buy. When the plants began to grow, he went over it again with DDT. He irrigated extravagantly, being what is called the *major domo* of the ditch commission, and keeping a wary eye on our little trickle of water. And in the fall there was no denying that he had the most abundant crops in the community. Truck after truck rolled away filled to the point of instability with the green alfalfa hay. He deposited box after box of dead ripe tomatoes at our kitchen door that first summer to be put up on shares with him. He roasted mounds of green corn in his huge outdoor beehive oven. There was no denying his success — nor his complete lack of understanding of what we were trying to do.

Not that we had a particularly clear understanding ourselves. We simply had a vision of what we wanted the land to look like — rich, dark, crumbly soil inhabited by healthy earthworms and yielding up prize fruits and vegetables. Restored fertility. And given our scant resources, we didn't do badly. But to fulfil that vision on even a few acres would have taken a lifetime of hard work.

Like Hawthorne at Brook Farm, we soon began to lament that man was made for more than this. Of course, there were many who took up the refrain before they had even tasted the "brutalizing" hard work. The few of us who were the first arrivals had set to work at once. We had brought with us several flats of carefully nurtured seedlings to be transplanted immediately since it was already the first week in June. But with the cat sleeping on them in the van, they had not survived the trip too well. Then Mr. Suarez donated some lusty tomato plants to us, beside which our own looked tubercular.

That first morning we awoke to a whistling wind sweeping up all the rain that had washed the hillsides so clean the evening before. Choking yellow dust filled the air and it was cold enough to wear the heaviest clothes we had brought. Faye and I set about unpacking and cleaning indoors while Jack, Wayne, and Bob worked down in a field Suarez had recently plowed. We could see them from the house, leaning into the wind, trying to spread cottonseed meal on the iron-locked land. They came in chapped and raw themselves, overwhelmed with the futility of their work. We waited till evening when the wind died down to set out the plants.

Nothing much ever came of that garden. It sat on the dry slope, impervious to our unskilled attempts at irrigation. We refused to use commercial fertilizer, much to the bewilderment of Mr. Suarez. By July the area where the cottonseed meal had been spread was a lush green strip of bindweed with the most brilliant scarlet blossoms ever seen in that part of the country. Every species of insect in the county flocked there, but once again we refused insecticide, again to Suarez's consternation. It seemed to him that we were deliberately thwarting the agricultural process. His patch of corn, which we undertook to hoe in return for his having plowed up our field, flourished, while ours was withered and stunted. It was then that we set to work on the spot below the irrigation ditch with pickaxes.

But by then the agricultural experiment had been so disappointing that very few had any interest in investing in another piece of recalcitrant ground. Wayne, who had grown up on a farm, would hoe the cornfield, but working in a kitchen garden was not his idea of farming. Daniel would put in a few hours by way of an anthropological experiment, from which he concluded that earthworms were the wisest of all creatures since they could eat the dirt itself with no need for a middle man. Bob had worn out his enthusiasm that first windy day and was only interested in engineering a less primitive irrigation system. Don was waiting for his karma to come the right way round so he wouldn't unsettle the plants. Most of the others, except for Lillian, hardly knew the top from the bottom of a seedling and distinguishing a bean from a weed was beyond them.

Our theoretical hope had been to live outside the dollar economy that enslaved us to the mass-produced fruits of big business. We wanted to grow our own food, construct our own buildings, and in the end become a self-contained community that could ride out any apocalypse in style. With what we considered unusually farsighted prudence, we made up lists of articles we knew we couldn't make in order to collect them against the day when Abernathy's General Store should no longer be operating. Needles and salt headed the list.

Nevertheless, no matter how indisposed any of us was to hard day-long work, nor how unskilled and futile our attempts at farming and building, everyone was surprisingly generous with his or her money. We operated off of the savings accounts of two of our number who had had regular full-time jobs the year before. But whatever other supply of money trickled in, from families back home, part-time jobs in Santa Fe, hidden hoards, it was shared with astonishing nonchalance. This was as much an outcome of affluence as was the inability to stick to hard, grueling work. Money came, and went, easily. When decisions about large expenditures had to be made, they were all quite content to leave it in the hands of Jack, Lillian, and me, the chief contributors.

Although we frequently and out of necessity used the services of the local public health clinic, for some reason it never occurred to us to apply for food stamps, even though over half the population of the valley lived on them, until we were down to our last few dollars. That came during the dead of winter. Jack and I, as usual, were the ones subtlely elected to do the applying. There had been much public controversy that year over how the government welfare agencies were to deal with communal applicants for the services. Therefore, rather than undergo the inspections and interrogations necessary for us all to apply as a household, we decided to apply only for ourselves and our children.

The four of us climbed into the frost-covered pickup one pale winter morning and started out for the county seat thirty-five miles south. We had heard that it was necessary to take along the children to prove their existence to the sometimes skeptical examiner. The idea of all that gratuitous play money that could be exchanged for real food filled me with childish excitement, and we were in a holiday mood. The children made up imaginary grocery lists as we bounced along.

The building was an old house converted into small offices and a waiting room guarded by an officious Chicano woman with an elaborate hairdo. Several other people came and went as we sat waiting in the stripped-down room, thumbing through back issues of *Cosmopolitan* and reading the latest USDA publications of economy recipes. I grew more and more offended as case after case preceded us. At times like this my theoretical radicalism flared into pragmatic confrontation. It was obvious that the bustling receptionist, so busy pulling out drawers and snapping letterheads in and out of her typewriter, found us even more distasteful than most welfare cases. After all, we should know better. We were deliberately subverting the system. We were clearly capable of finding employment if we'd only go back to where we came from. And for our part we had just enough shame at receiving anything, especially something as essential as food, at the hands of a government we castigated, that we were edgy with defensiveness. Naturally we had gone over all the arguments in our favor — how we had contributed so many tax dollars so unwillingly over the years to the governmental coffers, most of which was spent against our expressed wishes for war machinery. We knew that the food stamp program was primarily a ploy to keep agribusiness booming with customers that otherwise would not be able to buy their products. Yet these exposures were painful and humiliating. After an hour and a half, the children grew restless, and I no longer demanded that they sit still and look at the magazines. Instead, I smiled maliciously as they raced around the small room and climbed on the furniture. We were the next ones to be called in for consultation.

The office we entered was a lean-to washroom that still held an old washing machine in the corner. The man behind the battered desk looked both unhappy and apprehensive. His black hair was slicked back in an outdated pompador above a high narrow forehead. Dark heavy glasses hung sadly on his nose. His crisp white shirt ballooned around him, divided symmetrically by a dark tie. He was obviously unused to dealing with gringo food stamp applicants, most of whom were further west or north from his county. He was as polite and deferential as the receptionist had been haughty and rude. He explained the current rules to us thoroughly and filled out our application without comment. The children leaned silently against us and stared at him with big, uncomprehending eyes. It had always been their father and mother who were the ones dressed up in nice clothes asking questions of nervous students. Now things were turned around. It was hard to understand, both for the agent and for them.

Our application had to be processed, and it would be another two weeks before the U.S. Department of Agriculture decided to sprinkle its largesse upon the poor inhabitants of our county so that they could swamp Safeway with the little colored coupons.

Two weeks later was a somewhat warmer morning. We only had to drive the five miles to the local village this time, but when we arrived the line had already extended itself outside the abandoned adobe building which was now put into use only for the monthly food stamp distribution. It was awkward again. The village people refrained out of politeness from staring at us, at least when we were looking their way. There was an expectant, almost festive air among them. They were mostly women except for an unattached lone man here and there. Food stamp day meant relief, in more ways than one. The past few days had been spent eking out the last of the beans and masa. Tonight there would be canned spaghetti, canned peaches, sliced white bread.

The line inched forward, place being given to the oldest who had to sit on the benches that lined the wall. As we passed through the doorway, there was the same sad man we had seen in the county seat, dressed in an immaculate green suit and white shirt, wearily dispensing the pink booklets and checking off the recipients in his ledger. He did his job about as well as anyone could. I'm certain he heard many a hard-luck story in his daily rounds, both real and fabricated. Massive poverty is hard to hold up against. Shame and anger must be his daily lot. I hoped he found at least an occasional, if ambiguous, satisfaction.

A rail-thin old woman in a flowered voile dress covered by a sagging black cardigan shuffled to the counter in her felt house slippers and held out her boney brown fingers as he counted the coupons into them. "Dice, veinte, treinta. . . ." His grandmother might very well be standing in a similar line today.

Domingo, one of the town drunks, his face scrabbly with a two-day-old grizzled beard, blinked at the booklets and made an X beside his name in the ledger. Outside the building he was already looking for someone to sell them to for cash, the only bar-acceptable currency.

The housewives watched like hawks as their allotment was counted out, then recounted them carefully before signing the book. They collected their small ones hanging on their skirts and made off without further ado to Abernathy's to pay off the bill they had run up last month and start on a fresh stock of canned goods.

We moved up to the counter. "Dice, veinte, treinta. . . ." He caught himself and began again. "Ten, twenty, thirty. . . ." We signed the book briskly and made off in the pickup to the county-seat Safeway, where the lower prices more than made up for the gasoline expense. Fortunately, we were not tied to Abernathy's. Oh the glories of cheese, canned sardines, pickles, and crackers. By noon we were munching away contentedly in the park, wrapped up to our eyes against the wind and watching the children at recess across the street.

It was not long before I too adopted with ease the attitude of the village housewives. While standing in the food stamp line was galling for Jack, it was as natural as

Assault on Eden   71

going to the laundromat for me. I watched the booklets counted out as closely as the other women, though I never quite had the effrontery to recount them right under the sad man's nose. At the check-out stand in the supermarket things were a little touchier, and I did glance around to see who was behind me in line before I took out my pack of booklets. But the chances were 50-50 that they too were paying with food stamps. There is a certain female ferocity that goes with food-providing that precludes any possibility of humiliation.

On the way home that first day, we passed a herd of goats grazing beside the highway on the open, rocky hillside. An old man in a poncho that hung down to his knees was herding them. He leaned on a long pole and watched us pass, staring as long and imperturbably as one of the stones that covered the land around him. No matter how many times we passed the old man in our comings and goings, it was always the same long, slow, open stare that he gave us. No sidewise glances or surreptitious looks. He had become as nearly as possible like the land about him, with no reason to disguise his interest or amazement with what passed him on the highway. That dark, strong face had passed beyond every humiliation, beyond every pretense.

We got back to the farm in time to encounter Wilson. Wilson had a face in many ways like the old goatherd's — lean, sunburned, and stoney — except that its look was often sharp, quick, and contemptuous. Wilson was our benefactor. We all called him that as though it were an official title. He owned the farm we lived on. Born and raised himself on an even more barren farm somewhere south of us, he had nurtured a dream for years of coming back to this familiar landscape and putting his many talents to work. His mind was continually buzzing with schemes for building, engineering projects, jewelry designs, paintings. Yet he had been trained to an academic profession which he felt paid him too well to give up yet. He had suffered several tragedies in his life, including the loss of his wife, and he tried in an impatient way and with the stolid aid of his mother to bring up his three children.

He had decided to lend us his land without ever having laid eyes on us. This was all negotiated through a mutual friend. Over the weeks we had built up a romantic picture of this generous, trusting benefactor. We had been living at the farm almost three months before we met him. Generous he had indeed been. He would have lifted an ironic eyebrow at the "trusting" and called it foolhardy. In his impetuous way, Wilson was willing to enter into almost any exciting scheme, the more dramatic the better. But he could not abide failure. It rose like an acrid smell in his long, autocratic nose.

When he heard that the garden had withered away, he sighed a long weary sigh. When some of the rabbits sickened and died, he breathed an almost audible prayer for patience. When repairs to the house came to a standstill for lack of funds, he stomped around the place pointing out improvements that could be made for no cash outlay. He would breeze in on a Saturday afternoon long enough to satisfy himself of our continued incompetence, and then drive off again in a cloud of ill-concealed disgust. We were all left feeling like ungrateful children.

We had often challenged him to give up his tiresome administrative job and come live on the farm to provide the skill and leadership we so distinctly needed. To this he would smile benignly and shake his head. "Someone has to *pay* for the place, you know." Another cloud of guilt burst over our heads.

Wilson had bizarre economies. He never used butter or margarine, insisting loudly that bacon grease was quite sufficient as he poured it in great quantities over his pancakes. His children told us that he refused to have a refrigerator during the winter, leaving things out in the garage to freeze. He used cooking oil to slick down his sparse grey hair. He had an ancient Plymouth station wagon overhauled and then had it reupholstered with custom-made leather seat covers.

He was such a strange combination of so many opposites that at first we were simply fascinated by him. He had all the exaggerated personality distortions of a character out of Dickens. It didn't take long for the fascination to wear thin, however. Soon Jack and I were left by the others to deal with Wilson as best we could. Whenever he appeared in his whirlwind way, everyone drifted outside or into the dark corners, leaving him with his boots propped up near the wood stove and we two trying to strike an appropriate pose somewhere between jocular camaraderie and accountable foremen of a worthless crew of ne'er-do-wells.

Wilson liked to think of himself as one of us. "I know that everyone thinks I do nothing but live high on the hog," he would say with an injured tone, "but it's only to pay off this place. And I've my old mother to provide for. I'd give it up in a minute to be out here. Just think of me as one of the bunch though. I certainly don't expect any obsequiousness." And he would stare dolefully into the fire.

This evening as we rolled in, a light, feathery blanket of snow already covered the ground. We hoisted the boxes of food from the pickup bed, eying Wilson's little Corvair with apprehension. The yellow light fell out the kitchen door onto the snow; it would have warmed our weary hearts had we not known what waited us inside. As we lumbered in the door with the high-piled boxes, which ordinarily brought the whole crew dancing around us in anticipation, only Sally looked up at us blackly from the stove where she was stirring a stew. Wilson was bustling around the kitchen, opening cans of what he thought would be a welcome addition to the pot.

He stopped momentarily to investigate our new food hoard. "Peanut butter?" he queried, holding up a three-pound jar. "I should have thought you could make that in the blender using real peanuts. And white sugar! I thought you people were health food nuts. Here, Sally, I think it's time for these to go in now." And he handed her a jar of pickled artichoke hearts he had brought along as his personal contribution to the meal.

During supper, an uncomfortable enough affair owing not only to the pickled artichokes swimming beyond their depth in the midst of the carrots and turnips, we began again our long assault on Wilson to allow us to use the irrigated fields in the spring. Suarez had been leasing them ever since Wilson had bought the place.

"Really, Wilson, I don't see how you can expect us to do anything without water." Jack's voice was getting a rough edge to it. "We only manage to get a trickle for the garden because Suarez is the *major domo* and winks at it since he's afraid he'll lose the lease on the alfalfa otherwise."

"Yes, that Suarez is crafty, isn't he." And Wilson chuckled with appreciation for our thriving neighbor. Obviously, he was more impressed with Suarez's solitary success than with our poor scrabbling efforts.

"If you really believed in what we were doing . . . " Jerry for once spoke up, determined to push the point home.

"You misunderstand me, you misunderstand me." Wilson held up a defending hand. "What would you work it with? You've no equipment and heaven knows I've no money to be buying any."

Everyone held his breath, hoping that Jerry wouldn't say horses and bring up an even more unpleasant topic. But he only muttered something incomprehensible under his breath and attacked an artichoke savagely.

Wilson went on. "Now I know you're all thinking I'm against you and don't trust your abilities." He paused long enough for the point to sink home that he would be perfectly justified in such opinions. "But after supper we'll walk down the road to the river and I'll point out to you a strip of mine that has been approved for irrigation, in fact already has a ditch to it and a gate."

However, the group that assembled outside the kitchen door after supper included only Wilson, Jack, Jerry, and me. The others had had a full measure of Wilson's magnanimity and were creeping in by the fire as we set off down the lane, now obscured with snow, towards the river. The whole world seemed suspended in a steely blue light, the light of a snow-diffused twilight. The flakes fell thickly on our caps and hunched shoulders and our boots kicked up feathery clouds of white dust. It was a beautiful night. The whole sky seemed to be in a continual state of falling. A white world closed in.

Of course, when we got to the strip Wilson had been telling us about, we could do no more than mentally mark its position in order to come back and examine it later. The snow was piled high but we could tell by the fence posts that it was a rather small strip, no more than two or three acres.

All of a sudden the dogs put up a tremendous yelping and barking. They were lunging and backing off from a dark shape we could only just make out near the fence line on the road further down. We waded through the gloom to investigate it. There, barely discernible through the dark and drifting snow, was the stiffening hide of a donkey, one we recognized as having spent the summer grazing in Suarez's alfalfa. "What's this!" I cried, meaning not what but why.

Wilson smiled crookedly and put out a gloved hand to touch the grey hide. It swung against the fence and the piled up snow cascaded softly down. "Suarez," he said, "kills a donkey every winter so his dogs'll have some meat." He nodded his head in respect to the farsighted Suarez.

I turned my back and we started the walk home. My toes were freezing in my boots and I felt frozen inside. All night long that stiffening donkey hide flapped against the fence inside my head.

Dante, exiled from his native Florence and forced during the last and most productive years of his life to depend on the charities of a patron, wrote of "how salty the bread taste in others' houses, and how hard is the going up and down of others' stairs." We too chafed under the restraint of not living on our own place. Decisions were frustrated; failure is a blacker fear if it means failing your patron. How we longed for one clear moment of unalloyed gratitude, to be able to say the word "benefactor" without the load of irony it carried for us now. Though we came to know every slope, every arroyo, every defiant plant that grew on that land, our love for it was forever unconsummated. It belonged to someone else.

Not that the land cared about such questions. But there were people in northern New Mexico who would have disputed Wilson's right to the property — proponents of the original land-grant theory who declared that the land ceded to them by the Spanish crown centuries before had been illegally taken from the Spanish settlers in shady deals by Anglos. And back behind that were the claims of the Indians who had been cruelly driven from the land by the Spanish settlers. They had not even the Western concept of land ownership to be defrauded of. The earth was their mother in a way that had degenerated into sentimentality for us. Yet the land had yielded to them as scantily as it did to us. Our shriveled little garden had more in common with the dry land farms of the Southwest Indians than with Suarez's forced bounty. At Mesa Verde are tiny ears of corn, preserved for centuries — the undeniable record of the returns given for patient tending.

Of course there was no question of going back to that sort of life on the land. Our senses have deteriorated far below the sharpness necessary to hunt and to gather wild food. Besides, the buffalo, the berries, the fish, had gone with the Indians. And no matter how romantic the vision, we would not recover it.

Our dilemma was hopeless. Small wonder the Robin Hood stories held the same appeal for us they had for the late Middle Ages, when the ideas about land ownership were also in flux. How lovely to return to the forest, living off its natural abundance and filling in the chinks with booty from the bad guys — a life with a great deal more flair than food stamps offered.

For us, there were no more Sherwood forests, only the daily butting our heads against the crumbling adobe wall of our benefactor.

6

You are dust and to dust you shall return.
—Genesis 3:19

We are dying, we are dying, we are all of us dying
and nothing will stay the death-flood rising within us
and soon it will rise on the world, on the outside world.
We are dying, we are dying, piecemeal our bodies are dying
and our strength leaves us,
and our soul cowers naked in the dark rain over the flood,
cowering in the last branches of the tree of our life.
—D. H. Lawrence, "The Ship of Death"

The sidewalk leading up the hill to the clinic was broken and heaved up by the frozen ground. I had to pick my way carefully among the thawed spots in the snow. I must take care not to fall.

The clinic was north of the courthouse and one of the newer buildings in this town, generally left behind in the backwash of progress. I knew by report that the woman at the reception desk was a dragon. If I could make it past her, there would be friendly, helpful faces down the left corridor, where the women lined up once a week for birth control pills and pregnancy examinations. As she pushed the forms across the counter to me, I could easily read the question in her eyes: why wasn't I where I belonged, on the other side of town in some cozy private waiting room? I swallowed at my nausea and tried meekly to focus on the forms before me. I was in no such feisty mood as I had been at the stamp office.

"Occupation: Beekeeper"

My mind plummeted back to an old-fashioned romantic novel I had read in adolescence, *The Keeper of the Bees.* Lots of warm hillsides and fragrant meadows. Not much about the interminable scraping of bee gum from frames, the angry hum of bees caught in the hair. Oh, for a sun-warmed hillside. Outside the plate glass of the reception room the bare branches swung in the early spring wind and the dirty slush hardened into packed ice. Would it ever be warm again?

The receptionist eyed the form critically, then glanced at me with a look that gave me to understand she didn't believe a word of it, and motioned vaguely toward the left corridor. I'd made it past the first barrier.

I took my place in the row of chairs that lined the hallway, thankful for a place to sit and breathe deeply. The walls were postered with pictures designed to educate the poor and ignorant about medical care for their babies — inoculations, vaccinations, emergency treatment for accidental poisoning. And information about various birth control methods. Fat healthy babies smiled down at me alongside diagrams of IUD's. I tried not to look at either one and concentrated on the women around me.

Some stared stolidly out over their swollen abdomens, sighing shallowly from time to time. Others remonstrated ineffectually with toddlers who played hide-and-seek under the chairs and accepted smugly the compliments from their neighbors on the bright eyes, the curly hair, the cleverness of their offspring. Still others sat smoking and swinging a nervous leg, eying the little bodies tumbling around them with marked suspicion.

The nurses hurried back and forth from room to room,

counting out pills, sticking needles in round little bottoms, explaining with extreme care the necessity of taking every pill on time. Brisk, clean, efficient. Why had I ever left that world, I groaned inwardly. I knew almost all the nurses. Each of them was widowed, their children gone from home. Devoted to their work, they found their duty plainly before them, simple and clean with few ambiguities. And so pressed for time they hadn't the luxury of introspection. The one who visited our village every month smiled as she whisked by me. "It won't be long," she said encouragingly. And it wasn't. No longer than the waits in the cozy private waiting rooms across town.

In the dressing cubicle I slipped shivering into a sadistic little plastic shirt. All around me in the other cubicles the women were talking back and forth and giggling at their predicament. I began to tremble violently.

It wasn't long till my name was called and another nurse ushered me into the examining room. The doctor, her face plain and comforting as a potato, indicated the table, and I scooted myself onto it.

"Now then, what seems to be your problem?"

"I, uh, haven't had a regular period in three months. Just some irregular bleeding."

"Let's take a look."

She pushed and prodded and poked at my tense body, all the time her eyes staring noncommittally across the table.

"I was afraid I might be pregnant," I began.

"No need to be afraid," she said. "You definitely are."

"But I *can't* be," I protested. "I've had an IUD for a year now."

"It must have transmigrated," she replied. "That happens fairly often. They're not foolproof."

"But what does that mean? That is, where is it and what . . ."

"It probably moved up through the vagina and is stuck somewhere in the uterus along with the fetus. How much have you been bleeding?"

"Intermittently. Not a lot. But will this damage the baby? I mean, is there a chance something will be wrong with it?"

She drew in her bottom lip and looked thoughtful. "The chances are good it will be perfectly normal. I can't guarantee it, of course. However, if you're concerned about that possibility, I can get you into Bernalillo County hospital. Only an overnight trip and it can all be taken care of."

"We hadn't intended," I choked out, "to have any more children. I thought the IUD . . . "

"I understand." She patted my knee. "It's up to you to decide. Really I think it will be all right. However, if the possibility upsets you, I can handle all the arrangements at the hospital. No trouble. But you must decide soon. The cut-off time is sixteen weeks and I think you're getting near that already."

"I'll let you know," I said weakly. "I'll have to talk it over with my husband."

"Sure," she answered. "The nurse will give you the usual vitamins and nausea tablets if you need them." And she hurried off to the next patient.

I picked my way even more carefully back down the broken sidewalk. Clutching the boxes of pills inside my coat pocket, trying not to think till I had made it safely back home. As I went up I had only been full of vague suspicions and annoyance. Now it was sure. Something live inside me, something to protect. All my other feelings would have to be sorted out later. Anger, fear, worry, disappointment, excitement, anticipation, hope. Now I only concentrated on getting down the hillside without slipping and falling.

Back at home, everyone thought the news immensely entertaining. Though all of them would have gone to almost any lengths to avoid being saddled with pregnancy and a child, they reacted with hoary humor to my predicament. The same old jokes and comments their parents and grandparents had made in similar situations were pulled gleefully for my benefit. Why people should react with such glowing and clumsy goodwill was beyond me. The possibility of impending abortion, however, was no laughing matter. But that was my problem and Jack's.

The matter was never much in doubt from the beginning. "She says she thinks it'll be all right?" he asked worriedly.

"Yes. Of course there's no way of knowing really."

"It might be a boy," he said guardedly.

"Yes. Perhaps."

"I really can't have the final say, you know." He wrapped his coat around me as we walked down the road to the river. "Whichever way you want to go. If you don't want to take the chance, I'm certainly with you. Or if you do."

I was several days deciding. If only she had said the chances were 50-50 it would be damaged, then my way would have been clear. But the possibilities seemed greater for a whole, well child.

I fought against it with every ounce of educated rationality I had. But there is something so tempting about secret, hidden, growing things. How would it turn out? What if it were a son? And the girls were excited too. I had cautioned them against assuming that everything was all right, explaining carefully all the potential hazards. Yet their eyes gleamed too as they looked at me expectantly. "We'll help, Mother. We'll take care of it." Probably I had already decided the morning I had walked so carefully down the hill from the clinic. I told the doctor the next week to forget about the arrangements at the hospital. She nodded and made a regular appointment for me the next month at the clinic.

Once more life was full of anticipation and hope. I no longer cared who came or went on the farm. I had my own secret concern. My body became of intense interest to me, every new sign of advancing pregnancy filling me with satisfied accomplishment. It was all right. Another day and it had grown a little more. The life inside me was like a sign of new hope, a new beginning. A child of promise.

The weather began to turn warm at last. The sun

moved daily higher in the sky from its winter hibernation in the southern sector. More minutes of light crept in at the end of each day. We began breaking the ground for the new garden.

The plans for the irrigated strip closer to the river had never worked out. By spring Jerry had left, his heart broken, and we had neither horses nor machinery to work it nor enough strong bodies to make up for the lack. But we were expanding the garden from the year before. All our efforts in our neighbors' corrals and at the city sludge dump were not going to be fruitless.

The winter had been full of sickness. Sally had had to go to Denver for an operation. She came back on the bus still shaky and weak. "I'd better get a job in town," she told us. "I'd be no good out here at all. I'm not strong enough to work outdoors, and I'd only be a drain on everyone else." We all agreed it was best for her to be somewhere that could be kept reasonably warm and clean. But we all missed her whimsy that kept us cheered. We had much rather given up Simon and his unremitting gloom.

Then sickness had struck us all. From the first summer we had all been troubled intermittently with severe diarrhea and nausea. Thinking that our problem came in by way of the flies that swarmed around the dilapidated outhouse, we spent several weeks during the first summer designing and building a new one — a lovely little A-frame with screens on the windows and a wooden floor. Blasting a hole out of the rock with dynamite had been the high point of Bob's New Mexico adventure. Nevertheless, although the sanitary facilities were much improved, the problem persisted. We all got periodically sick with fits of violent vomiting, diarrhea, chills, and sometimes fever. In fact, it grew even worse during the winter when all the flies had long since died off.

It was efficient Lillian who, after suffering a long bout herself, took in water samples from our tap to be tested by the health department. The report came back: paratyphoid. We investigated the source of our water supply. The well reservoir was full of all sorts of dead creeping things, including a mouse. But that wasn't the real source of the problem. The well itself was filled from the seepage of the irrigation canal and Suarez's horse pond, no more than twenty feet on the other side of our fence. The well was polluted. After this discovery, we hauled drinking water from town or boiled the well water. But the effects of paratyphoid are a long time getting over. By the end of the winter only our own family and Wilson's teenage son remained on a day-in, day-out basis. Others came and went. We had frequent visitors, sometimes strangers passing through, looking for a place to embark on a similar project themselves. But broken relationships between men and women and broken health had ravaged our original community.

Still I was hopeful. Our little family had grown tighter through it all. Let everyone else go! We knew we could depend on one another. It had been a year of hell — the poverty, the sickness, the cold, the hard work, the desertions — but we had come through. And now there would be a new one amongst us.

Jane, our seven-year-old, who had chosen not to go to school, was with me constantly. She watched the goats after I had staked them every morning below the garden. We spent sunny afternoons scraping the accumulations of bee gum from second-hand frames. "There are ten frames in a super. We've done seven already. How many more do we have to do?" I would ask. "We've put six tomato plants in each row and we've made three rows. How many is that?" "Enough," would be her obstinate reply.

Gradually the garden took shape. Out of our new hotbed I transferred small lettuces, cabbage, broccoli, and cauliflower in all shades of green. We mulched with straw against what we knew would be the dry early summer. Once again plans began to germinate in our heads. A new house. We could at least start on the foundation. There were free rocks and clay in abundance. We made up lists of honey customers and scrubbed out gallon jars in anticipation of the golden flow.

I didn't notice till I was standing at the sink over the

lunch dishes the dark red trickle down my leg. I carefully wiped it away before Jane could see, told her to finish washing up, and went quickly to the bedroom. I lay down on the bed and stared at the ceiling, my head spinning and buzzing. I didn't even formulate any words in my mind, didn't tell myself to be calm or not to worry. I simply lay there and waited, like any animal in danger waits alert for the next thing that is going to happen. But nothing more happened. I lay there for an hour, then turned cautiously onto my side and began to breathe deeply again and to plan. The next clinic wasn't for four days. What did this mean? What should I do?

Jack had been working for one of the local ranchers. When he came in late in the afternoon I sent him off again to the nearest gas station to call the nurse in town. "Have her stay in bed," she instructed. "And unless the bleeding gets any worse, we'll see her in clinic next Tuesday."

I stayed in bed and the problem seemed to disappear. It had only been a bad scare. At the clinic the doctor examined me, frowning in concentration. "It's still growing," she reported. "There's nothing really to be done. Just stay off your feet as much as possible. And if the bleeding gets bad, come into town immediately and the nurse-midwife will handle everything. She'll examine you and make the decision."

Shaken, we left the clinic and climbed in the old pickup. Jack carefully avoided every chughole on the way home.

Each day now there was only one question in my mind. Would we make it? I woke up every morning, checked myself for bleeding, tottered into the kitchen and sat down again. Then I fixed breakfast slowly, allowing myself no more than five minutes at a time on my feet. After the other children were off to school, Jane and I would go back to bed for another hour. If things were going well after that, we would scrape some more honey frames.

Watching Jack, almost dropping from weariness now

that he had all his work and most of mine to do too, I was torn apart with indecision. Perhaps I should have gone ahead with the abortion. We couldn't afford this invalidism. Maybe I should simply get up, continue with my part of the work, and take the consequences. Besides, my determined mind gave itself a shake, I'm a strong, healthy woman who has borne two other children with no problems. I'm simply overdramatizing the situation.

So one morning early in April I crept cautiously down to the garden. I worked all morning, setting tomatoes into the cold frame. Nothing happened. My heart lifted again. It was going to be all right.

The next two days I worked warily in the garden, irrigating, planting, hoping. On the third day late in the afternoon I stood up from patting down the final row of peas and blood gushed from me like a torrent, saturating my jeans and boots. "Quick, Jane, quick. Go get Daddy." I was crying and trembling and she seemed uncertain whether to stay or go until I screamed at her again to hurry.

I went doubled over up to the house holding the bulge of my abdomen as though to protect it from whatever was happening inside. I stripped off my soaked clothes and lay down shivering and sobbing under the blankets. A few minutes later and Jack was there. Alice had just come in from school and he set her to heating some water to wash me in. By the time I was cleaned up, the bleeding had almost stopped. I dressed, Jack left instructions for the children in case we didn't get back that night and we started the hour long drive into town.

It was dark when we got there. He rang up the nurse-midwife from a service station and she arranged to meet us at the clinic. There was no dragon to face this time, no waiting women lining the hall, just the dark clinic and one lighted examining room. The nurse shook her head. "It seems to have pretty well stopped now. And there's still a heart beat. Why don't you stay in town tonight, just in case, and I'll look at you again tomorrow."

Out in the dark street again, we held on to one another tightly, and considered. At least there was a temporary respite and some reason to hope. We decided to treat ourselves to a warm comfortable motel room with a real bath provided amply with hot running water.

Lying between the crisp clean sheets, knowing that if I swung my feet over the side of the bed and sat up, a curly carpet instead of gritty concrete would touch my toes, that I could walk into the bathroom a few feet away, see myself in a brightly lighted mirror and wash myself in gallons of hot water, in the midst of all this comfort that for most of my life had been my natural habitat, I began to feel that nothing could touch me here. Those horrible explosions of blood only belonged to that stark, uncontrollable world where things crept up on one — dirt, sweat, smoke, splinters, disease. Here we had the upper hand on life. It was safe.

I snuggled down under the blankets and slept, hour after hour, waking only when Jack brought in a sack of apples, cheese, and crackers. He had made a fast trip home early in the morning to see that the children were all right. Mrs. Chavez, a close neighbor, was keeping an eye on them.

In the afternoon I went by the clinic again. The bleeding had almost stopped altogether. "Go on home," the nurse advised us. "But stay in bed as much as possible." She was used to dealing with women for whom staying in bed all day was about as possible as flying to the moon. She didn't say it very hopefully.

I hated to leave the motel room, but I couldn't stay there for the next four months. And we had already spent more money than we could afford on this expedition. We bounced home, watching a perfect sunset. As we rolled into the yard, the kitchen door filled with three expectant faces. Are you all right? Have you come home to us? Their relief was gleeful as they saw both of us climb down out of the truck. The kitchen was a wreck from their efforts to get supper ready. We sat down to a boisterous meal. Jane settled herself against my side. It had been only twenty-four hours since I left. Here I was back again. Nothing had changed. The problems were still there.

This was not the last of the terrified dashes to the hospital, Jack shooting anguished glances at me as he geared down, eased over wash-outs in the road, and tried to make up the time on open stretches. Emergency room. Examination. Still alive, still a heart beat. Go home. Complete bedrest. This will have to work itself out.

For six weeks I was in bed almost constantly. Jane was my nurse. Quick, attentive, longsuffering. She read what books she could to me after I had grown tired of reading myself. I worked on house plans, drawing and measuring and re-drawing. When all this was over. . . .

Between emergency trips all was calm. The nurse had begun teaching us the la Maze breathing techniques, which we practiced assiduously. We all spent time searching for suitable names. This special child must have a special name. The girls described in inaccurate detail the care they would take of their baby brother. I smiled but did not encourage their fantasy.

I watched my body like a cat at a mousehole, ready to pounce on the least sign of hope or despair. I was hiding my own secret from myself. I closed my eyes and tried to concentrate on what was going on inside the dark cavern of my body. Surely I should know, should be able to pick up some echo from within.

I was worried. It didn't seem like it was growing as it should. At least I wasn't as big as I had been in previous pregnancies. Perhaps it was simply the lack of normal activity.

The spring came on, warm one day, windy the next. The bees were out, reaping every early flower. The peas Jack planted were up. Every day was one day closer.

On one of the windy days, I was watching the sand whipped through the air and the branches of the new-leafed trees bent straight out over the irrigation ditch when I heard a rasping, scrabbling noise across the room. Not a rat, I prayed, catching my breath. It was high up somewhere, almost on the ceiling. I picked up a shoe beside the mattress and waited, ready to heave it at whatever varmint had invaded my room. The noise stopped, then began again. Finally I saw it. A giant centipede, at least a foot long, was descending the opposite wall in uncertain fits and starts. Its weight was against it as it skidded from toehold to toehold in the rough concrete wall. I lifted the shoe and aimed it as well as I could from my bed. It hit one end of the creature, knocking it down the remaining length of wall where it fell in a bent heap; then it started skittering first one way and then another aimlessly. I screamed for Jane who was in the kitchen and quite unlikely to hear me. I was in terror lest the thing would find its way to the bed. At last Jane came in trailing her dish towel.

"Watch out," I cried, pointing to the centipede. "Get something quick. A big stick."

She ran outside to the woodpile, picked up a hefty chunk and came running in again. The prospect of getting close enough to hit it quailed her, however, and she simply hurled the stick at it with all her might and ran out to get more. By the time the broken body of the centipede had stopped its frenzied scurrying, the floor was littered with firewood. When it was over we huddled together on the bed and cried, at the twisted, twitching, hideous form, the fear, its long dying. We left it there till Jack came in, incredulous at its size, and removed it at the end of one of the sticks.

I spent more time outside after that, lying on the new grass under the trees. Waiting, waiting. There was nothing else to do. Some days I was hopeful; other times my mind was as dulled as any animal.

It was the middle of May on a Sunday. I had had some minor bleeding in the morning, only to discover the small, ivory-colored coil of the IUD had expelled itself. The bleeding stopped. At last, I breathed deeper, it's over, it's truly going to be all right.

I walked down to the garden and propped myself beneath a tree, planning what I would do now, how I could help. An hour later I began to notice small but unmistakable contractions. About twenty minutes apart I judged. I didn't even dare shift positions. I waited. They continued. Grew closer. It was midafternoon before I climbed slowly back to the house, checked the overnight bag I always kept ready, and sent Jack to call the nurse.

This was the last time, I knew. Wordless all the way to town, we held fast to each other's hand. We drew up in front of the hospital this time. The lawn was already filled with roses. The sun was heavy and yellow.

Inside the nurse was waiting. Sunday afternoon was slow and leisurely at the hopsital. I was put in a labor room this time, doing the breathing exercises and holding tight to Jack. "I'm not going to give you anything, not even an aspirin," the nurse-midwife told us. "There's still a chance the baby can make it. Only a slight one. It's so early. Still, we want to give it every chance."

I nodded, working hard at breathing right, catching the pain cleanly on its edge. Jack stood beside me, his eyes big and dark. "Now!" he would say, feeling my muscles tighten under his hand.

Two hours. The characteristic pause in contractions that occurs just before the big push. Jack rushed for the nurse. I was wheeling down the hall, Jack still rehearsing the instructions with me. The nurse and I disappeared inside the swinging doors. There was a bright light. I was shaking and cold. The nurse looked at me from between my knees which seemed like mountains looming up in white draperies.

"Push," she commanded. I pushed.

"Again, harder," she said sharply. I bore down hard. I felt like I was going to turn inside out.

"Push," she shouted. And this time with all my strength I pushed out into the world the secret I had borne for over half a year. I felt it slide inside me, give way, then rush forth, and with it a cry I hardly recognized as my own, tearing along my lungs, expelling the weeks of anguish and fear. It was only an inarticulate scream; it meant it's over.

She told me immediately. "It's dead," she said. "It was dead before it was born. A little boy. Very small."

She laid it aside and was busy delivering the afterbirth. I didn't try to see it. "Push," she repeated periodically. And I pushed between great heaving sobs. She said nothing more, but patted my ankle from time to time. When it was over she sent me away with another nurse.

My grief seemed to fill me up more than the child ever had. It was heavy and its bitterness unambiguous. To have come so close, to have lost what we worked for so hard. A boy. A son. I truly did not know how I could bear the loss.

Early the next morning I had surgery. It was shortly after dawn when the doctor slipped into my room. "Are you certain you want to go through with this?" she asked. "A tubal ligation is a very final thing."

"Yes. I couldn't live through another disappointment like this. I have my two children. That's the quota."

Friends came to see me, some of the old communitarians. I couldn't speak without weeping. They went away again. They think it's strange, I told myself. One less baby in the world at this point in history is only a blessing. I should have given it up earlier. I ground my teeth and choked.

Two days later I went home. I wept unremittingly. My parents came. I told my mother I could not bear it. She said I would learn how.

7

> So he drove out the man; and he placed at the east of the garden of Eden cherubims, and a flaming sword which turned every way, to keep the way of the tree of life.
> — Genesis 3:24

> Yet, after all, let us acknowledge it wiser, if not more sagacious, to follow out one's day-dream to its natural consummation, although, if the vision has been worth having, it is certain never to be consummated otherwise than by a failure.
> — Hawthorne, *Blithedale Romance*

Summer began again, full of feverish activity. The garden, three times the size of the first summer's, promised at least a fair crop. We extracted honey weekly now, taking turns at the crank handle and watching the golden liquid flow like a miracle from the spout into the gallon jars. And we worked on the house, hauling rock, tramping adobe in a mud pit, drying bricks in the front yard.

We had all three of Wilson's children with us now, and occasional passers-through. But I shrank morbidly from outside human contact. People were an almost insupportable burden. I saw vehicles draw up to the front gate with disgust and revulsion. "People are so predictable," I protested to Jack when he mentioned bringing someone new onto the farm. "It's never anything different, never anything new. Always the same petty stupidities."

My attitude angered Jack. It was ironical, I thought. Here was Jack, naturally gregarious, yet with a volatile, explosive temper that sometimes frightened people away, linked with me, who would outwardly put up with multitudes of failings while secretly despising people in my heart.

Wilson, who had scarcely shown his face during the spring, now came down almost every weekend, bringing friends with him. He had been put off by my pregnancy, making no attempt to hide his opinion that our decision against an abortion was stupid and senseless at a time like this. He never mentioned the miscarriage at all. The friends he brought were well-to-do, more often women than not, excited at the prospect of seeing a real hippie farm in operation. Strangely enough, I resented these people far less than the ragged regiments of dreamers that rolled into the yard to stay a day or two and scout around for a prospective paradise. I was contemptuous of their amorphous plans, the hope that glowed on their faces for a blurry, brighter tomorrow, the sentimental, bastardized Eastern mysticism they espoused. "You'll never make it," I muttered under my breath. "You're not tough enough."

I kept a daily, detailed diary, but it very purposefully contained only incidents of the nonhuman world. I saved accounts of the garden, the weather, the animals, the sun and moon, but I obstinately refused to let any human vicissitude enter the story. What people did or did not do was now beside the point.

In short, I was well on my way to becoming a first-rate Stoic. My credentials lay in my ability to take almost anything — 30°-below winters around a woodstove, disease, hard work, welfare examiners, dirt, disappointment, death. Nothing could touch me. I cultivated calmness in the face of calamity. My life belonged to me; I was responsible for it.

We worked hard through the summer, but still there seemed to be a blight on our efforts. Wilson, who at first had been excited about our new building plans, was now dissatisfied. "There's not the right amount of straw in these bricks," he protested. "They won't dry right that way." "You ought to haul rocks from further down by the river." I could see the handwriting on the as yet unfinished wall.

Nothing we did pleased him. He grew more irritable with each succeeding visit. We began to see that there was only one way to solve our hassles with Wilson: we must try to buy from him a few acres of the property where we could build a house in peace and release ourselves from this tenant-farmer burden. He was obviously shocked when we presented our plan to him, but promised to think about it.

One day a lone straggler appeared in the yard, his hair long and matted and his shirt thrown over his shoulder along with a day pack containing his few belongings. He had come from a commune we knew of further north in the mountains. A band of drunk local studs had invaded the place, killed one of their members, carried off one of the women in their car trunk and raped and left her not far from town. Everyone from there was leaving, fleeing. We fed him and he went on, not knowing where, following the road.

Meanwhile, a school friend of ours from the midwest, Margaret, came to stay for a while. She had with her a hitchhiker she'd picked up while camping in a national park. "This is Keith," she introduced him. "He's from Florida. He teaches English in a junior college there. And he's published some poetry." Keith was big and muscular, eager to make himself useful. We mentally assessed the number and size of rocks he could haul in a day.

After supper he told his own story. "I'm just sort of knocking around now. I lost my family. My wife and two little girls were killed in a car wreck last spring. I'm just trying to get it together again."

We were shocked that anyone could sustain such a blow with such equanimity. "Sure, you can stay," Jack told him. "I know you don't want to be making any permanent decisions now. But unload your gear, we'll put you to work, and you can see how you feel about it after a while."

Keith was rather rough, especially with Wilson's boy, and I found it difficult to think of him in any poetical setting. But this wasn't the nineteenth century, I reminded myself.

And he worked hard, sticking with the job all morning long, then ready to go again after lunch. One day he asked to borrow the van; he had some errands to take care of in town. "Sure," Jack agreed. "We'll see you this evening."

Keith returned late in the afternoon. He'd bought some old work clothes at a second-hand store.

I was relieved to have an extra pair of hands around the place. Visions of the new house standing snug and warm by the first snow flickered through my mind as I watched Jack and Keith unloading the rocks at the new site. I wasn't happy with Jack's response to Keith, however. They were together constantly, talking, talking, talking. I only hovered around the periphery of their attention, squaw-like. I'm not enough for Jack, I thought. He needs something more. Other people. It made me angry to think that he found Keith's company so congenial that they sat up every evening till after midnight while I went to bed alone.

About a week later, when Jack and I were down in the garden hoeing, a big white car pulled onto the bridge. "Who's that?" I asked warily, shading my eyes against the sun. We were sometimes harassed by cars full of drunken villagers out on hippie-heckling excursions. Jack turned to look. A man in a dark uniform emerged from the car. He waved and came toward us. Jack propped his hoe against the fence and went to meet him. I continued hoeing. I had no truck with policemen around here. I watched them move on up towards the house. What could it be? I counted off all the possibilities in my mind. Search? Someone we knew in an accident? What? I kept hoeing till I saw the car drive off, then rushed up to the house. There was no need to ask. Everyone was around me trying to speak at once.

"You'll never believe it," they gasped. "It's Keith. They took him away. His wife — she came for him."

"But . . . she's dead," I protested.

"Didn't look like it to me, the way she grabbed him."

When Keith had seen the police drive up, he had ducked into the big bedroom, Alice told us. He had quickly changed into the clothes he had come in and stuffed all his new old clothes into his backpack. He had come out again then, as if prepared for what was going to happen next.

Meanwhile, Jack said, the policeman had shown him a picture of Keith to identify. "He's not under arrest or anything," the policeman assured Jack. "It's just that his wife's looking for him." Jack had been startled at the woman in a tight pantsuit and piled up hairdo who was just getting out of the car. She looked old enough to be Keith's mother. "Says he disappeared about two weeks ago."

At that moment Keith opened the kitchen door and came slowly down the steps, his eyes on the ground. By the time he reached the gate, the woman had thrown herself upon him. "Oh, Keith honey, where have you been?" He put his arms rather reluctantly around her and they moved off to the car.

Jack was finally shaken out of his amazement enough to run after him. "Hey, man. What shall we do with your things? Don't you want to take them with you?"

Keith shook his head, still unwilling to raise his eyes to Jack's. "You keep 'em," he said in an undertone. "Maybe I'll be back."

With that they all climbed back into the big white car and headed off towards town.

That was the last we ever saw or heard of Keith. In his backpack we found a classic letter, written to his wife but never mailed, explaining how he had taken their money out of savings, how she would undoubtedly hate him, how he felt compelled to do this. We inherited the fruits of the savings account — an expensive backpack, a down sleeping bag and an alpine tent. The letter had not been addressed, so there was no way of returning them.

"I don't think he wanted her to know he had them," Margaret said. We were still sitting around the supper table, stunned by the scene. "Gee, you guys, I'm sorry. When I brought him here I didn't know . . . "

"No way you could have," I said. "How strange. Of

course he never had been a teacher. Or a poet." I felt relieved about that.

"Or a father."

It was a little scarey that we had been so easily conned. Even I, with my deep-rooted suspicions of human nature, so well watered by the past year's experience, had not been able to spot the deception, even when all of us had openly wondered at certain incongruities in his actions. Here I thought I had built up a wall of skepticism around myself that made me invulnerable to almost anything. And I had been taken in by a stupid, obviously fabricated story. I wasn't careful enough yet.

Jack's concern was elsewhere. "I wonder what'll happen to him now."

"He'll never get another chance, that's for sure," Margaret said.

The incident with Keith shook us badly. On its heels came another shock. Alice was going to have to have an operation. "Just a simple hernia repair," the doctor assured us. "I know your circumstances are somewhat," he paused and arranged the pen beside the telephone, "straightened. I'll only charge half my normal fee."

It was generous and I thanked him. But even half the fee was money we didn't have. Family-planning and maternity clinics were one thing. A ten-year-old with a funny lump on her otherwise flat little belly was something else. We couldn't forever depend on the public services of a county already overloaded with poverty.

I was frantic as I drove home. It was *my* life. Why wasn't I able to control it better? There must be a way. My mind darted down one path after another. At the end of each was either a wall, a dark question, or the lurking monster that wheezed, "Give up. Leave. It's over."

That possibility made me tremble so I could hardly drive. "No!" I almost shouted aloud. "I will not. I can not."

Every evening now was spent going over the tortuous

paths that opened out from our present standing place. Borrow the money for the operation from our parents. An obvious defeat. Borrow the money from Wilson. We choked on that one. He hadn't even mentioned again our offer to buy a piece of land from him. To borrow would be like shopping at the company store. Finally: get a job. That meant leaving. At least one of us. The farm was too far out from anywhere to commute. And what kind of job? The unemployment rate in the county was eighteen percent and upward. We had managed to get by during the summer on our honey sales and food stamps. Now what?

Jack ran his hands through his thick dark hair and sighed. "I guess we better go into town tomorrow. See what we can find there." He got out a suit that had been packed away in plastic for over a year. I ironed a dress and unearthed some stockings. The girls danced around us and clapped their hands. "Gee, mama, you all look just like you *used* to." We grinned grimly at one another.

Our first stop was at the hospital. Through the ever active but seldom precise grapevine we had heard there were openings for social workers there. We filled out the application forms in the corner of an office, full of hope, then saw the secretary stack them with almost an inch of other similar applications. "We'll let you know," she said, closing the door behind us. Outside the air was full of the first tinges of the thick golden autumn sunlight. Among the flower beds the insects droned heavily, nearing their end. Any day now there would be a freeze.

We sat in the truck staring straight ahead but making no effort to move for a while. "What next?" Jack asked.

"There's an ad in the paper for a secretary at the college," I said. "And an assistant in the library."

"Okay. I'll drop you off there and go on over to the welfare office. They seem to hire almost anybody."

We made our separate rounds. At the college, the personnel manager was cordial but shocked that someone with a master's degree should be applying for a secretary's job.

"It's been our experience," she said, tapping the paper before her with her pencil, "that underemployed people aren't happy with their work for long."

"Underemployed?"

"Yes. People who have more education or qualifications than the job requires."

"Better underemployed than unemployed."

"Perhaps," she answered vaguely.

Jack's experience at the welfare office had been as unproductive. "I filled out the forms, but there was a backlog a mile long." We chugged mournfully along the road home.

The next day Jack went further afield to Santa Fe. "Don't wait up for me," he said. "I may have to stay over to get around to all the places."

I spent the day hoeing in a desultory fashion, picking a few beans, watching the bees crawl over the last of the clover. But everything seemed to fall from my hands after a while. One cannot grasp hold of work firmly when one is expecting it to be snatched away at any moment. By evening I had settled into a dull torpor. What was happening now, across the mountains in Santa Fe? Any luck? Any job? The prospect of leaving the farm was enough to unnerve me. But what if no job at all appeared? What then? We were, at long last, at the end of our rope.

The night was long. I watched the moon rise and make its arc across the blackness above, as I had lain by the window and watched it often before. I always knew now just what phase the moon was in, something I had never noticed much over a year ago. It was a strong light on our sonorro, often strong enough to cast shadows and efface the light of the stars around it. If I had to leave here, the moon would be taken away from me.

It was dark again the next evening before Jack came pulling into the yard. His suit was wrinkled by now and the knees had smudges on them. "Car trouble," he explained, "as usual." I set before him the supper I had kept warm in the oven and waited. "No luck," he said. "At least nothing definite. I went to every school in Santa Fe. Even the prison. They had an opening for a teacher there. But I don't think. . . . Maybe . . . " He got up and went outside, leaving his supper half finished.

The next day we didn't go anywhere. Jack suffered the same ennui I felt. He would pick up a stone and then let it fall in confusion from his hands. Would we ever live in that house? It didn't seem worth the effort to do anything at all. So we sat in the sunshine and tried to think of new ways of phrasing the old question: what shall we do now?

In the afternoon one of the little Chavez girls came timidly up to the gate. "Can you come to the telephone?" she asked. "Someone wants you." We both sprung up, vacillating between hope and fear.

"I didn't give the Chavez phone number on any of the applications," Jack said. "What can it mean?" He dashed off down the road after the little girl. Thirty minutes later he came back whooping. "A job," he cried. "A job!" A friend of ours, knowing our plight, had suggested us as consultants for a federally funded project in town. A short-term affair — only three months — but good money while it lasted. Almost physically the weight of fear fell off us. The children laughed and shouted. I began mentally to pack.

The next day was Sunday. Some friends from a farm further up the river came and took the goats away. Maisie was just as obstinate about leaving as she had been about coming here. But after we coaxed her two curious golden children into the back of the truck, she followed, albeit with much complaining. Matilda had to be cornered and carried away, a job that took most of the afternoon.

After the truck had rumbled away, we wandered up behind the house and sat down on an old wagon bed that was slowly disintegrating into the landscape. The sky was pink in the west. In the greying east the evening star grew brighter. Suarez's truck, surrounded by its phalanx of dogs, stopped down on the bridge. He crawled out and stood gazing down at the water, now flowing higher than at any time during the summer. Having satisfied himself that all was well, he climbed back in, whistled to the dog that rode beside him, and the truck lumbered slowly on home. Further down the road, the sound of the Chavez children playing in that final hour before bedtime came drifting pleasantly along the dusty road. This was my home. That first spring night I had lain awake in the dark, wondering where I was, had drifted backwards into the past. Now I knew this place as I had never known any other: all the trees, the weeds, the insects and animals. I knew the hard, reluctant dirt and how the water ran over it. When it would rain, when it would snow, when the wind would beat the dust into the air. When the river would turn muddy red and when it would flicker clear over the round rocks in its bed. I had filled notebooks with its description, a daily diary of weather and earth doings. Now it was over and gone. Or rather my sojourn here was over and gone. The sun would continue to go down over the purple mesas, the evening star glow in the east, and Suarez check the water in the ditch. But I would not be here. I had learned where I was only to leave it. To the land itself I had only been a passing acquaintance. It would shrug off every imprint of our story soon. Only the beginnings of the rock walls would remain, looking as much like ruins as beginnings.

Within a week we were packed and moving out. Wilson came down to see us off, angry and accusing. He insisted that we leave everything we had acquired since we came there, taking only what we had brought with us from the Midwest. We were too worn out and overwhelmed with failure to argue with him.

"I should have known it wouldn't work," he said. "You're running out. Giving up."

"Wilson, we've tried to explain. There's this operation of Alice's. And you've given us no assurance about the land, that you'll sell any to us or make any arrangements."

"You expect me to make agreements with people who give up?" he cried.

We knew then that it was hopeless, had been hopeless from the start.
    The morning we hauled the last load away was bright and clear. We shut and locked the door and whistled to the dog. We bumped out through the gate and shut it again slowly, drawing the barbed wire loop tight over the skinned pole, savoring for the last time the sun soaking into the dry sonorro. We pulled past all the scattered adobe houses with the hollyhocks turning brown in the front yards. Out on the road a band of lean stray horses tore up slender mouthfuls of dry buffalo grass and stared at us with large, unconcerned eyes. They didn't have to leave. Sparse as their life was, they didn't have to leave.

8

> Then he showed me the river of the water of life, bright as crystal, flowing from the throne of God and of the Lamb through the middle of the street of the city; also, on either side of the river, the tree of life . . . and the leaves of the tree were for the healing of the nations. There shall no more be anything accursed.
> — Revelation 22

> But now the detestable, gangrenous suburb I have to walk through, the workers' shacks with their peeling paint and permanent layers of dirt, the tool sheds sinking into the sewers and streams that reek of washing and toilets, and the corrugated iron that constitutes man's choicest building material — all are gone, transformed into a wall of pure gold, a new enclosure for the city, pierced by the river of living water, as by an eternal crystal.
> — Jacques Ellul, *The Meaning of the City*

When we had set out toward our new life five seasons before, we imagined that we were driving our pale blue pickup straight into the heart of the beatific vision. It had been to us a simple matter of escaping the wrath to come by reentering the Garden of Delight. Whenever anyone has said "back to the land," what they have really meant is "back to Eden." Back to that union with creation from which we have been severed but for which we have retained a taste through centuries of starvation. Even now, when we are further removed from that union than at any time in human history, when only artificial environments are familiar to us and the "natural world" has become something strange and exotic, even in this pitiable state the craving for creation is stronger than ever in our hearts. So strong that we were ready to risk all we had, or thought we had, to slake that thirst.

We had, however, failed to reckon with the cherubim and the flaming sword. Somehow for our age it is easy enough to believe in Eden, that repository of all pleasures of which we have ever had an inkling and where the twisted ambiguities of our lives are straightened out. But cherubim remain ridiculous to us. Instead we have a comic St. Peter perhaps, acting as tour guide through those dusty reliquaries of jokes about heaven. But militant angels to exclude the enlightened? Where was the fairness in that?

If our parents — call them by whatever names you please — Adam and Eve or Mr. and Mrs. Middleclass — had fallen, made mistakes, chosen badly, how could that affect us? We couldn't be blamed for their transgressions. Yet when we came smack up against the gates to the garden, not only were we turned away, but the blow from the flaming sword still smarts to this day. We weren't simply refused admittance; in our attempt to storm the gates we were doomed to reenact every area of failure pronounced upon our forebears. It was our story the Yahwist was telling in Genesis.

We also, just as Eve, desired a tree to make us wise. This was in fact the very temptation to which we yielded in what is comfortably called "drug experiences" nowadays. We voraciously sought vision, insight, knowledge, through many labyrinthine ways — astrology, I Ching, yoga, fasting — and the result was always and ever only more self-consciousness. We discovered the same truth over and over: that we were naked. Defenseless, powerless, exposed to assaults from an inimical society and ungovernable nature. Treachery and betrayal between friends and lovers, brokenness — untogetherness — within. The same curse that descended so graphically on Eve and Adam when they desired to become wise overwhelmed us also as we ingested whatever chemicals we too had invested with that magical aura of illumination.

This is not intended to be a polemic against — or for — hallucenogenics. Like everything else in the natural world, like yoga or meditation or diets or fasting, they are merely raw material. They operated for us the way the Law worked for Paul in Galatians. They gave us knowledge of our inadequacies and nakedness. That knowledge in itself is of very little value. Adam and Eve were better off before the necessity of fig leaves. The consciousness of one's own nakedness can easily lead only to paranoia, fear, distrust, contempt for the nakedness of others, especially if they're not quite so conscious of their condition as you. Simply because we had an avenue to self-consciousness that most of our society was fearful of venturing upon (the appeal the serpent made was to venturesomeness), we were contemptuous of those who denied themselves this vision of their nakedness.

True, one was also given from time to time visions of surpassing loveliness, of intricacies and grandeur in the natural world humming around the self-conscious mind. But these visions in themselves made impossible demands upon the seer: if the flow of life so lovely to behold was to go on uninterrupted, one must remain absolutely still so as not to break in upon the flow and destroy its natural pattern. As soon as we moved we were an intrusion, outsiders upsetting perfection. Thus the hours' long vigils on rocky hillsides watching an anthill, hardly daring to breathe. As soon as the vision was over and one stood up, an entire cadre of insects was crushed underfoot. To a cow coming along behind and wiping out whole communities with complete abandon, this was nothing, but to those cursed with self-consciousness, the knowledge that one is a misfit was a continual bitterness.

Perhaps the healthiest wisdom we attained through eating of the cannabis tree and related species was the ridiculousness of our position. How many hours we spent around the table, around the stove, trucking over the rough ground, laughing like loons at ourselves and our complete incongruity in this world. Seeing the kitchen as a television stage, the sonorro as a movie set, memorizing Firesign Theatre records. Everything was at least two removes from reality. It was hilariously funny, this dislocation of ours, and the tree of knowledge showed us just how funny.

And sometimes it showed us how scarey. How tenuous was our out-of-place foothold upon this earth and how little it mattered to the buzzing, humming universe whether our foot slipped or not. Our breaking our necks falling from a cliff or drowning in the red water of the river was of as little significance ultimately as our disruption of the anthill. The cosmos would go on with its exploding and imploding imperturbably. Eden had operated admirably, after all, without Adam.

What if the animals had had no names? The creatures had flourished nameless. Maisie and Matilda, Big Mama and Peter certainly loved us no more for all their foolish names. They resisted us till the iron bar was laid to the back of their skulls or we shut them into someone else's truck and gratefully took the unresisting money in exchange. The enmity that was placed between humans and the rest of the animal world was not resolved at Moriah. The fact that it had to be lived with and accepted as a part of agrarian life did not heal the breach. The cages, the fences, the ropes, the bee veils and smokers, the sporadic attempts at vegetarianism were all testimonies to an ambiguity and an oppression we had inherited.

To a generation infatuated with a Disney World version of St. Francis, this curse of hostility between them and that part of creation most like themselves, what we call "intelligent life," capable of communication (the serpent could speak), was especially difficult to bear. Of course, we see it most forcefully, as did the Genesis story-teller, in the enmity of those creatures most unlike ourselves — the scaly, cold-blooded, legless serpent. But the hostility was no less in the six-legged bees with their fury of efficiency. We went about bruising one another as often as our paths crossed. However, the furrier and warmer-blooded the creatures got, the more disheartening was that barrier between us. How to live so that this distrust and animosity was overcome? Small wonder that one of the marks of redeemed creation is the cohabitation of the lion and the lamb, and that we humans should be partners to that treaty. Yet at Moriah we never found St. Francis' secret. The creatures relentlessly resisted us.

But our sorrow was tempered by one faint hint of something we had hoped was not an illusion — freedom. Every animal we caged had the innate urge running through its ever expectant sinews to escape. The watchful, unblinking eyes, the kicking and biting and struggling all gave us hope. These creatures, uncursed by self-consciousness, incapable of falsifying reality and deceiving themselves, brought us, as Walt Whitman put it, "tokens of ourselves." Freedom was not an illusion; it was a reality ardently yearned for by these creatures so similar yet so hostile to us, their jailors. They kept the flavor of freedom alive for us too.

In a world as deterministic as ours, it is easy not to believe in freedom anymore. Yet it was more than anything else the taste for freedom that had called us out of the cages we had lived in so acquiescently. We wanted to break out of a society where the choices had already been made for us by shadowy powers that filled our feeders and water dishes regularly but checked the latch on the cage door just as unfailingly.

Choices and alternatives are not efficient. They slow down the machinery and make trouble for those responsible for keeping the wheels rolling. Yet it was the complicated and time-consuming sideroads that fascinated us. However, it was not only the rigidity of a relatively recent technological society that kept us bound. There was lacking an inner freedom in our relationships with one another, a repetition of ages-old patterns that we seemed unable to break.

Nowhere was this more startlingly evident than in the

relationships between men and women. That we were somehow aware of this particular curse showed through in our studied attempts to overcome it. Theories and practical regimens for solving what the men called "the woman problem" multiplied and were modified daily. Friendships were possible; indeed they sometimes flourished, particularly between people of the same sex, drawn together by common interests, similar backgrounds, mutually compatible personalities. But it was exceedingly difficult for men and women to be friends, much less lovers, with any long-lived success, due primarily to the suspicion and jealousy born of possessiveness. There was rarely even the simple sensual pleasure of reciprocal sexual desire. The object of passion was more often than not completely oblivious to the subject, or else twisted the situation to his or her own advantage.

This, I believe, was especially bitter for the women. If they were unaware of or unconvinced by the curse in Genesis, they were quite uncomfortably aware of Freud's restatement of it: Biology is destiny. If they had succeeded in circumventing the first part of the curse — in grief you shall bear children — the second part still rankled enough to produce profound misery. The dilemma was this: any man, given the chance, would "lord it over" a woman. Yet in satisfying sexual desires, how does one avoid opening oneself up to that distinct possibility? Desire, fear, and resentment tore at every woman there. The more exotic alternative — notably lesbianism and nymphomania — we were at least clearheaded enough to recognize as fraught with as many dangers as plain old vanilla sexual exploitation. We may have talked bravely about settling for "mere sex," but when the moment came, we all found it impossible and not really satisfactory to disentangle our affections from our genitals.

Men, I think, are usually unwitting pawns in this particular curse. Of course, we recognize that this Genesis story was first spoken in a culture which without much thought relegated women to the status of property. Which makes the story all the more fascinating. If there had not been some supracultural revelation that women were indeed responsible moral agents, how could they ever have played such a large and tragic part in this primeval drama? As regards the curse upon Eve, Adam merely acts out his now "natural" inclination to oppress. But if this is the "order of creation" in its paradisal state, we would have to say that enmity, grief, and shame were also a part of paradise. The oppression of women by men is a curse to be cured, not a creation to be glorified.

Nevertheless, it was not cured at Moriah. It festered, produced divisions and distrust. And it was one of the principal causes of our dissolution, because the insatiable desire for true sexual union went on unabated by one disappointment after another. When all the possibilities were exhausted within the community, it was time to move on and out. And for the pair of us who were linked together as one flesh, it was time to move on and in. Biology was indeed destiny in a way Freud perhaps never suspected. The ancient curse had to be dealt with day by day.

And day by day there were mouths to be fed. And work to be done. And of course there were those who refused to put their hand to the plow perhaps because they were already looking back.

If there was ever a land that sprung up with thorns and thistles, it was northern New Mexico, armed with cactus and cockleburs. The curse on this land was so glaring as to be obvious even to us. And much of the curse was the direct result of the interference of man. This barren country had not always been so. It was the Western Europeans who had laid it waste, just as the Africans had made a desert of the Sahara. And it was we, unfair as it was, who labored under the burden of their rapacity — sweating, stupid of the ways of the land, only slowly learning how to bring forth anything other than thorns and thistles.

And the curse on the ground didn't end there. This land we loved even in its barrenness, that we slowly learned to work with, was at the last denied us. That illusion that the earth can be owned infected both our vision and Wilson's, as it had Don Juan Oñate's before us. Friendship and community were destroyed by the accursed concept of possession.

Is it not the ultimate unfairness that, down with us, we should have dragged the rest of creation, despoiled it of its original beauty, made it merely an attribute of ourselves? Actually, the greatest virtue in living on the land is the way it makes one aware of our true state outside the garden; we live at the mercy of the rest of creation, dependent on it. It is easy enough in a city apartment to live as though we had indeed subdued the very weather. The farmer at least knows better.

In reading over various fantasies of Utopias that have from time to time beguiled the human imagination, from Plato's *Republic* to Skinner's *Walden Two,* I am struck by what is the central concern of them all — the division of labor and the ownership of property. They have all rightly identified property possession as a great evil, corrupting the basis of human community. All devised schemes for circumventing this evil. Plato proposed a "royal lie" to be told to the growing crop of guardians, that is, that they themselves grew out of the earth and are made of gold and therefore have no need of property that satisfies the common herd. Voltaire had the idea of making chamberpots and fetters out of gold and silver to reduce their value, and H. G. Wells made the World State "the sole landowner of the earth." Yet all these schemes seem incredibly naive now.

And the problem of work is an even bigger muddle among Utopians. They at least have had the clarity to see that property ownership is in itself unnatural, even if their cures are quackery. But of work itself, specifically identified as a curse upon humanity by the Genesis storyteller, who was hardheaded enough to see that one's very survival depended upon *someone's* unrelenting labor — of this curse the Utopians have sweated to make a virtue. Work is not a matter of amusing oneself, as Francis Bacon would have it in his *New Atlantis,* where the Renaissance scientist, dressed up as Solomon, putters around his laboratory. At least B. F. Skinner is realistic in prescribing more work-credits for disagreeable drudgery than for titillating research. Work is not prayer; it is one of those things we have learned to call so glibly a "necessary evil." For it is not the exertion of muscles nor the devouring of time that is at the heart of this curse, but the stark contingency of our position on this earth. We must eat. We live on a treadmill of necessity. No fruit drops, unaided, into our hand. Even the hunters-and-gatherers of this world, the aborigines, live in such an attenuated Paradise that few of us would share it with them.

Although those idlers who sat in the house all day at Moriah playing records or telling jokes on the front steps were ignorant of the Shorter Catechism, they were not fooled into thinking that the chief end of man was work, even if they were more intent on enjoying themselves than on enjoying God.

But then Utopias have always been rather dull affairs with no room or time to spare for idlers. Their designers feel acutely the mess human society is in. They have taken account of the dilapidated ruin into which we have fallen. But their answer has been a nail here and a patch there in an attempt to shore up the ruins, to make failure impossible. And with it that taste for freedom. There is another strange thing about Utopias: they are almost always discovered through some shipwreck or time-machine malfunction. Or else, as with Plato or Skinner, they are the result of sheer futurology fantasy. But the most ideal human societies actually discovered and described by anthropologists and attested to by old-fashioned empirical evidence, say the Mesolithic Caribou Eskimos of central Canada or the recently unearthed Tasaday tribe in the Philippines, where gentle concern for the common welfare is put before all else, who of our famous Utopians would go and join them? Their, and our, reluctance to do so would no doubt spring from some small quibble about dirt or diet. Land, food, and work. The curse has seemingly not been laid with equal severity on all peoples. Here and there in hidden places on the earth exist these dwindling bands of gentle humans who accept with humility the fragile precariousness of the space they occupy. But expose them for only a few days to the infection we bear and see which is stronger in this world — sickness or health.

In the end it is the dust that owns us all. Some peoples, usually those who have not sought to insulate themselves from the contingencies of life, submit to this final, uncontrollable happenstance with a grace we find difficult to understand. The stoicism I had trained myself in at Moriah did not serve me well when it came to death. It was easy enough to be stoical about the limp rabbit bodies that Jack so deftly skinned. Even if the sight was unpleasant, we always managed to eat the tasty flesh. The unsuspecting donkey that had gone to feed a pack of dogs, however, we saw as a mute accusation of our acquiescence in death. But the centipede scrabbling down the wall was nothing to me once it was broken to ineffectual bits. The dead baby bunnies we buried in the compost heap with perfect aplomb, congratulating ourselves on our stern stoicism. But when death crept nearer and reached its stilling hand into the very spring of life, our philosophies were undone. The birth of a dead child was the final contradiction, the last denial.

Yet with the curse there is always mercy that makes life possible, even in its brokenness. If Adam and Eve insisted on knowing their nakedness, God provided the clothing to cover it. The action is not cancelled, merely made bearable. With Eve's pain, he multiplied her pleasure, and if work is not a virtue, it is at least at times a consolation. Thus the curse is tempered and made barely bearable. We also were played out on a line, allowed to imagine that we had escaped the exigencies that affect ordinary mortals, and then with a snag that tore open the skin of our dreams, we were hauled back in to gasp the chill, harsh wind of reality that whistled through our inadequate gills.

A month after we had left Moriah and moved into a rundown but respectable neighborhood in town, we had struggled to our financial feet with the aid of our federal project jobs. Yet we were still spiritually desperate. Our agrarian dreams had dwindled to the size of our bare, packed-dirt yard where we half-heartedly sowed some grass seed. Our one remaining rabbit, poor Furball, was stolen by neighborhood boys and rescued down by the railroad track at the very moment they were about to hit it over the head with a bottle. The glorious autumn that had been full of high winds and apple picking and harvest the year before now filled only the narrow sky above our house. Our dog, ignorant of city ways, was run over and injured. Our friends were scattered, some of them still sick, almost all as disconsolate as ourselves. We were outside the gate, the sword at our backs, but not knowing which path to take away from the garden.

The house echoed with its emptiness. Without our discarded furniture and possessions, we hadn't even those familiar consolations. It was in every way a shabby and makeshift life. Sensing that this could only be an interim, a breathing space between the failure we'd left behind and an unknown future, our girls were uneasy and troubled. What next, they asked mutely.

Jack and I felt secure only at work, where everything was scheduled and programmed. But at night we couldn't sleep and clung together in the darkness, full of fear and anxiety. We were at our last extremity. We didn't know the answer to our children's question.

Alice had her operation. She was frightened, but as was her habit, tried not to show it. I sat by her bed and watched her come groggily, mistrustfully, out from under the anesthetic. While she was recuperating impatiently at home, I read to her in the afternoons the whole series of the Narnian books of C. S. Lewis, stories of a marvellous kingdom beyond our grimey time and space where adventure and heroism were continually enacted amongst true friends within a lovely land. The children could not devour enough

Assault on Eden 115

of these stories — Lewis says that youth has a natural appetite for heaven — and as for me, my own jaundiced palate began to tingle again with the longing for Something More. If only I too could somehow slip into a world where something mattered again. When we came to *The Silver Chair,* I recognized the sensation of living underground for so long that the sun itself seemed a myth. The torpor and cynicism that had bitten deep into Prince Rilian had settled into my bones too. I thought of Dostoevsky's underground man. Better not to live than be like that.

The Paradise I had lived for I had followed into the desert and found to be no more than a mirage. I couldn't stand a second disappointment like that, and besides, I had nothing left with which to stake a second claim. All my resources of every kind had been exhausted. Jack and I were exceptionally gentle towards one another but with the sympathy one invalid might have for another.

About three blocks straight down the street from our house sat a church we had often passed, initially as the town's first hippies, later as honey pedlars and clinic visitors, and most recently as respectably disguised researchers for the government. The name of the minister on the signboard was Gotheim, one I had often mentally sneered at — so obviously a German name in so overwhelmingly an alien culture. Other than that, I had given the building no attention at all. But now that my desperation was acute and no other path presented itself, I decided to venture down the three blocks — as tentatively as possible, just in case another painful disappointment should be lurking in the little white stucco building.

And really, what else could I expect but to have my suspicions confirmed? This or any other American church was no more than a travesty of certain high principles since betrayed by centuries of distortion and neglect. What was the use of even wrestling with the question of whether or not Jesus was who he claimed to be? What difference had it made if he were God himself or in some mysterious way related to him? It hadn't made any difference after all. Here was everything I valued on the brink of destruction, the forces of Evil so palpable one could feel them crowding in and smothering him. Surely Evil would ultimately collapse under its own weight; that was its nature. But after that what? Nothingness? Annihilation? I believed in Evil as I believed in nothing else. Its power was apparent in our own failure. We were helpless against it. Had not even Jesus been so?

Still, whether from desperation or the hunger sharpened by those children's stories, I decided to try this little church. No, it wasn't even a conscious decision, just a growing resolve.

If the gathered faithful ever caught a sense of the wild, desperate hope with which outsiders from time to time approach their familiar sanctuary, perhaps they would recapture a sense of dangerous deliverance instead of the all too frequent coziness or boredom that settles over them as they slip into their pews.

But no one could have told, of course. I said nothing at all to my unsuspecting family, simply got up on Sunday morning, put on my most unobtrusive career clothes, and made myself presentable for Presbyterians. When the girls learned what I was planning, which I finally had to explain with considerable embarrassment, they were excited at the prospect of this new experiment, not realizing with what trepidation I was setting out, far more than I had started for New Mexico with. They insisted on dressing up too and going with me. Jack said nothing, only looked at me with bewilderment. But when I reached the middle of the last block, I saw him coming along behind us, his hands thrust deeply into the pockets of his grey suit and his head down. We reached the church just as the ushers were closing the doors after the last stragglers and the music had begun.

To describe that place today is like trying to describe the details of one's first realization of home. It was being at the bottom of a deep well. It was dark and the sounds echoed.

And the well was filled up with half-forgotten associations that had collected and distilled over months of Sundays: the self-conscious swish of best clothes, the polished, dark-stained pews, the ornate iron heat registers, the careful sacred silence broken by whispers and coughs and crying babies, the chilled church air gradually warmed by the gathering bodies standing, sitting, pumping out the Gloria and Doxology.

People gather nowhere else on earth in the same strange spirit as when they worship. The air was charged with a multifold attention struggling to direct itself, to be taken up into, if only momentarily, Something More. The polka dots on the dress in front of me filled me with strange elation. The shoulders shifted under them and then straightened. Who knew what problems this woman brought with her, who exposed her nakedness despite the polka dots, to the one who walked in the garden at evening and said, "Where are you?" She had three boys sitting beside her who alternately poked at one another or turned and stared at us. When we stood to sing, the youngest leaned against his mother and she absently put an arm around him and patted his shirt front in time with the music.

The songs were like water in my parched mouth; I wrapped my tongue around delicious words that had to be drawn a long way up from the well of my memory. No one there, I felt, made the responses — "Lord, have mercy, Christ, have mercy" — out of such a deep wound as I did.

There was nothing extraordinary about the service, no trendy gimmicks to appeal to the disaffected. The traditional hymns were played by a graying organist. The choir was enthusiastically dreadful. I can recall neither the text nor the sermon, except that the words of the scripture affected me like one who has not heard his native tongue spoken for years. It was not slogans, not jargon, not rhetoric nor the deliberately leveled communication of the professional proletarian. It was language, elevated, elusive, drawing the hearer on and into its depth.

In contrast to the exalted words of his predecessors in a long chain of witnesses, the minister groped and stumbled, shifted syntax in mid-sentence, mispronounced, and muttered. Yet that detracted nothing. He was obviously excited about what he was saying; he attempted to hide none of his deficiencies and, what was more, seemed not a bit dismayed by them. They were entirely beside the point. His own nakedness had deepened to transparency.

It was all over too soon, the rustling bulletins, the hymnbooks plopping in the racks at the final threefold Amen. We shuffled through the handshaking line, the children staring up in frank wonderment at the unfamiliar faces. The minister was not the thin, pale missionary type I had expected, but rotund and red as any Martin Luther, his open black robe snagged at the sleeve and frayed at the collar. People were naturally curious about us, but they concealed it with as good a grace as possible so that our paranoia was not as excoriated as we had braced ourselves for.

It was the first salve on our raw sores we had felt in many a day. I tried picking about, as we walked home, for signs of a false comfort that came from once more having been among the secure bourgeoisie. But besides the fact that several people had seemed definitely on the outskirts of financial wellbeing, I was simply enjoying the release from my own torturing anxieties too much to do any analyzing.

We were, in fact, all disgustingly, Sunday-afternoon happy. The girls skipped ahead of us like something out of Dick and Jane. Jack and I had a long leisurely afternoon nap.

We went back that night for the potluck supper, carrying our contribution of two loaves of freshly baked whole wheat bread. This time I was more scared. It was one thing to sit in a church service among these people and quite another to sit at a table, eat a meal, make conversation with them. They all seemed quite jollified at passing through the line making inane comments about one another's supposed gluttony and piling their paper plates with each other's macaroni casseroles and green chili and chocolate cupcakes. But they were the insiders, used to the well-worn jokes and able to identify each dish with its maker. The waves of common humanness that washed about them, however, lapped up against us too. We sat with a biology professor and his wife. They had grown children, he told us wryly, folding and refolding his napkin, off somewhere seeing the world, experimenting. The conversation was awkward but possible. Somehow I made no unreasonable demands upon it. I felt sorry for these parents, resigned to not understanding their children. They were as real as I was.

This was only the beginning, of course, of a life together. Just so, lovers look back in amazement at their first meeting and laugh at the silly, inconsequential things that attracted them to one another. Fortified with food and fellowship with people we had long ago written off as insignificant, we walked home in the brittle autumn darkness. After we put the girls to bed, Jack and I talked, hesitantly, awkwardly about the day and its experiences. There was no denying its genuineness. There had been no razzmatazz to attract us with its innovativeness; just a certain stark homeliness. No back-slapping exuberance that I remembered only too well from earlier times, but a courteous curiosity and openness. Was it possible that in such an unlikely place lived a health stronger than our sickness? We were almost afraid to hope.

We felt as if we were emerging from the underground and discovering, somewhat like Prince Rilian, that the Son was not a myth after all. And our first inkling of this was the light and warmth we had felt that day. No matter what the theoretical pros and cons of such an unlikely story as the defeat of Death and the prospect of living under blessing rather than curse, we had that day touched, heard, eaten and drunk its evidence. To deny the mending and healing we could feel at work within us would be to deny our own senses.

We were as avid to follow this new hope, once we were

convinced of its authenticity, as we had been to follow our dream to New Mexico. We asked the minister to visit us, and when he did, assaulted him with a barrage of questions and information about our predicament. I think he was surprised at finding other people as excitable as he was, to whom faith in God's gracious and powerful purpose was a matter of life and death. Had all we had been through not been, after all, in vain? Had it been necessary for us to travel those subterranean ways in order to emerge in this place?

It is hard for anyone whose life has begun again to contain — or sustain — that first joy. The sense of living in a cosmic drama exhilarates, almost intoxicates. We say we want our lives to have meaning. Yet when the fact that this is so dawns upon us, we can scarcely stand under the weight of the implications.

Neither was the journey over. If we had always, unbeknownst to us, been on our way to this place of recognition and clarity, it was itself but a point on a pilgrimage that stretched before us. A pilgrimage that is absolutely unpredictable. Just like Bunyan's Christian on his journey, we were faced with the same decisions all over again every day. The underground portion of our quest was part of a pattern that did not end with a final flourish that Sunday in October. Following that we had a year as hired hands on a mountain ranch where we recollected ourselves, read, and became more inquisitive than ever before about our faith. During that year, the knowledge grew in us that the next step on our journey was seminary. Another three years there to work out how we were going to give an account of the hope that was in us. At one time, four years would have seemed an eternity of waiting. The apocalypse was already upon us. But the true relativity of time is revealed when one finally realizes that he is not writing the script to the cosmic drama, merely acting out his part in fidelity to its author. Last week the same biology professor with whom we had sat at that fateful table was the first to lay his hands on Jack's head at his ordination.

Last week also, Patricia Hearst, Emily and Jack Harris, and Wendy Yoshimura were arraigned in California courts, members of that other apocalyptic community, the Symbionese Liberation Army. I look at their pictures, read their statements, follow with fascination and fear the unfolding of their story. Because I know that the same road that took our caravan out of the Midwest several years ago could as easily have ended in the court as in the sanctuary. If the failure of the previous generation has been a lack of commitment, a lukewarmness, that particular sin has been matched by the kamikaze dedication of their children, who seem willing to risk anything for a few years' or even a few moments' confrontation with reality. The bliss of putting ambiguity once and for all behind one, of having the enemy finally focused and identified, is not to be idly disparaged. The flame of their unfeigned rage against an unjust society has become their funeral pyre, a holocaust in its ancient religious sense. Just such zealots, advocates of righteousness violence, were numbered among Christ's own disciples.

The question must be put clearly: Did a failure of nerve cause our revolutionary spirit to dwindle out in the desert? Only a fraction more of separation from society, perhaps a permanent disavowal from a parent, a solitary act of arrogant authority by the police, an unwarranted arrest, only one straw more and the social contract between ourselves and American society would have been irrevocably broken and we too would have become guerillas in an underground army for whom to die violently is itself victory. We too would have sought to lay hold of the Kingdom of God by violence.

But it was thin spidery threads of grace that averted the final rupture: the concern of the public health nurse, the obvious mental anguish of the food stamp official, even the postmistress at the next village who gave us her windfall apples. And also our own fear and revulsion for irrational violence, which was a more or less constant threat to us at Moriah, whether from drunks who cruised around the back roads in their own desperation or from businessmen sweating out their fantasies in their cars and hoping to pick up a compliant hitchhiker. Society was our adversary as surely as it was Noah's. And it was only through those unnoticed accumulations of small graces that we were restrained from attacking our adversary with the weapons it knows and understands only too well. The kingdom of this world is expert in violence and perverts to its own ends those who seek to attack it with its well-worn weapons.

Despite the dangers, there was something of solid value in the Moriah experience, even with its futility, dead-endness, and despair. It provided a stark and unavoidable confrontation with anguish, with unmitigated failure, that in other situations can easily be lied about, covered over, or distracted from. It made clear to me what being an exile from Eden means in a society that pretends, simultaneously, that there is no such place and that we have never left it.

I also learned some remarkable things about myself. For example, I had always pictured myself as easygoing and undemanding, the world's most inoffensive person. At Moriah I learned differently. I made tremendous demands on people. Contracting to live in the same household with me was like entering a monastery, only the rules were sprung on the unsuspecting novitiates after they had been led to believe they were on a holiday cruise. I demanded renunciation of all other loyalties, consecration of all one's energies to my particular dream, recognition of my superior discipline and austerity. Pounded daily upon the solidity of reality, my own image of myself began to crumble. I was someone very different than I had thought. One would suppose that this kind of learning could be a little easier come by. But if I had not had seventeen people instead of three telling me what I was like at close quarters, perhaps I never would have learned. Illusions break up on the rocks of reality, and how fortunate that they do. If we were writing the story ourselves, what a sad little meaningless tale it would be.

We learned another very important thing at Moriah: how to be poor. Poverty is viewed as the single greatest sin in our society. It is an enemy to be annihilated, a shame to be hidden. Whether springing from the conservative sources that say success is a sign of God's favor or from liberal sources that say we must all enter the heaven of the median income, the message is the same — we must be saved from poverty. But one has experiences when one is poor that are forever denied to insulated society, hermetically sealed in security. Of course, like anything else, like drugs or education or geography, poverty is raw material. It can be just as easily subverted as wealth, making its subject spiteful, petty, twisted. But in our society, the positive potential of poverty has been obscured. We scoff at its romantic advocates, pity its victims, ignore its Teacher.

I learned from poverty what I could have gone to no other school for. I learned not to rely on possessions to supply an identity. When you drive up to the bank in a rattletrap truck with slick tires and try to cash a check that you pull out of a worn flannel pocket with fingers permanently blackened with soot and axle grease, you learn to be prepared for people who don't believe in you; yet even against that heavy wall of denial, you know your own worth. You learn to stare down the insolent eyebrows of other customers who pay cash when you pull out your foodstamps, refusing to accept their ignorant estimate of yourself and knowing that we all ultimately live by welfare and grace. And, if you are very lucky, you learn how close to the edge human life is lived, how we are held in existence from moment to moment by a power we don't control. You can rejoice in life as a gift. In poverty there is no pretense and no protection.

The church became for us the fully fleshed reality of that phantom community that had always receded just over the horizon, always eluding our grasp. The amazing thing was that it was inhabited by the same sorts of dreadful people who had wandered through Moriah. Untrustworthy, petty, irresponsible, lazy, bad-tempered, demanding, manipulative. On top of that, most of them were decidedly middle class and had no aspirations to be otherwise. Quite a few drove offensively large cars, ate meat without a qualm, and were Republicans. Some were alcoholics; some were neurotics; some were simply boring. Still they came together regularly for the specific purpose of being judged. Their failures and inadequacies were weekly pointed out to them. They were exposed, naked before one another. And though they writhed or sighed or denied, they seldom fell into despair, accepting with joy or wry bewilderment the mystery of forgiveness that was just as regularly placed before them.

They were a redeemed community, or at least they were continually told they were, even if they didn't often feel like it. And if the full realization of their redemption lay in the future and was as yet only dimly perceived, still there were enough flashes of fulfillment and foretaste to keep alive the hope. A chemist scoffed at the moldy notion of angelic choirs in heaven; he was the choir director. Alongside him was a Chicano volunteer worker on welfare who sweated out his own private chemistry of alcoholism. There was an old maid schoolteacher, fretful in retirement, afraid of falling on her stairs and not being discovered for days. The couple facing divorce over the heads of their unsuspecting children. And the old, grime-encrusted, palsied half-wit who showed up Sunday after Sunday, shovelling in quantities of food at the potlucks; he was there because it was a place where he could shake hands with half a hundred people who knew his name.

None of these were people I would have chosen to set up an "intentional community" with. Few, if any, shared my radical political views. They were confused, frightened, pained by the chaos and change that whirled them around like flotsam in its rush. But their reality was as solid as mine and the community we all formed together was more solid than any of us.

Christians today experience a very meager diet of communal life for the most part, a few hours a week at best. There are those enclaves, especially among Roman

Catholics, of a few who, having tasted liturgical community, seek something more. Thus we have monasteries, convents, Protestant and ecumenical communes of various sorts. What of their efficacy and future?

Donald Bloesch in *Wellsprings of Renewal* (Eerdmans, 1974) has described a veritable smorgasbord of contemporary Christian communal efforts, manifesting a multitude of tastes. But to enter upon any of these ventures is an exceedingly dangerous undertaking. To enter a monastery, one must take a series of vows, graduated in their seriousness and timespan. No less serious should be the commitment of Protestants entering a communal discipline. It will be a task more difficult than anything the novice has tried before. If one is having trouble with his marriage, he shouldn't try to assuage the pain by entering a commune, which is a magnified marriage. If one is dedicated primarily to self-development or personal growth, he shouldn't join a commune, where the survival of the community requires daily crucifixion of private desire. The body cannot long sustain an overgrown eye or ear or foot unless it is to become a monster.

I would almost say no American should enter a commune. We have been trained for competition, personal achievement, rewards, outstandingness as a way of life. That cultural conditioning makes up such a large portion of our personality that we would be a gaping hole without it. If that hole is not filled with a substance stronger than cultural conditioning, the effort will be futile and guilt-ridden.

I must warn myself against this great and dangerous discipline of communal life. The discipline of being a part of an ordinary church, one that periodically appears and disappears like atomic particles, is almost insupportable for all of us at times. Locally we are torn by such petty considerations as what color to paint the kitchen or whether or not the choir should process. Globally we are torn by the same stupid questions put to Jesus by the first disciples — where shall we find bread for the multitudes and what do you mean by the Kingdom of God anyway? I can foresee a lifetime of learning to live in this querulous community.

In fact, to face the final humiliating truth, as long as I have my own family, I don't feel the need for anything more than those intermittent flashes of community. Hell, says Sartre, that preëminent existentialist, is other people. Heaven, replies C. S. Lewis, is an acquired taste. And some of us have to go through Hell to get there.

"The Kingdom of God is hard enough," I protest, "and now you pile on top of that the Body of Christ. What do you expect of me anyhow?"

"Something more."

And how do I explain my life now? When exactly, at what point, did it become different? Does the little girl baptized on her eighth Easter so many years ago have no part in this story? Was her act unconsidered, of no account, not efficacious? Or did it mark the person I am forever, no matter how I tried to conceal, slough off, disguise my inscribed identity even to myself. For at no time did it occur to me to actively renounce that Christ I had been baptized into, just as I would never have renounced a friend who had given me no cause for harm, though I openly mocked the disfigured representations of him I found everywhere about me. I was a lost sheep wandering through the valley of that dark shadow, but one who had been branded at baptism with an ineradicable mark.

One can with perhaps more rationality attribute the reversal of my life to the early childhood education I received in the church rather than to the mystical experience of baptism, and I would be the last to discount it, although I am not at all sure that what I learned was what the Sunday School thought it was teaching. Furthermore, my life at home was often only torturously Christian, not at all the Dick-and-Jane model in pabulum pastel colors that was the unattainable aspiration of several generations. What I learned in church and what was grafted to me by my baptism was radical behavior. Unconventional giving-up-everything, throwing-it-all-over behavior. And though I lost almost everything else except a vague, buried sense of loyalty to an absent Friend, I never lost that.

I have in this story tried to chart the nadir, to isolate the lowest point on the graph and the moment when the line began its upward movement. Certainly the story is now often full of great gobbets of pure sweetness. At times I sustain a continual state of gratitude, often for days on end. Great joy springs from this current of gratitude which is at the same time wonder at my life and its continuing creation directly from the hand of God.

Yet doubtful, depressed, unfruitful interludes interrupt this flow. I would not be mapping this Christian path with the painstaking accuracy it demands if I denied that. There are times when all the beauty and bliss of early morning light being taken into a glowing curl of orange peel and shimmering on the skin of steam hovering over the coffee cup is, by some horror, changed into smears of mess and disorder, husks from which the meaning has been sucked. At such moments, which stretch themselves into days, even weeks, the line on the graph plummets off the page.

I call these the times of obedience, when we are left without a reason why, without a meaning, just as Eve had no real reason given to her to explain why she shouldn't eat the fruit of the tree of knowledge. At those times we don't remain obedient in order to feel joyful or fulfilled or positive or anything. Usually we are capable of feeling only a dull ache at best. We remain faithful, even though the words we pray are dust in our mouths, because we have a Lord of our lives, not a beneficent Behaviorist who doles out rewards for positive reinforcement.

And now, instead of the boredom of empty Sunday afternoons, fullness of life, sometimes to the point where one staggers under its weight. Boredom is not depression but flight from it. It knows nothing of battles with dark forces because it will not stay and fight. Indeed it has no reason to fight, no weapons to fight with. And if the lives of my own particular saints are any indication, there will be an age of fighting. Luther's later years were filled with his worst depressions; C. S. Lewis' last nights with terror and nightmares.

But there are also now the times of protection and praise. We have in our house healing and a communion that is holy. All of us, even our animals, rejoice in one another. We say often to ourselves, "Isn't that just like her?" or "You get that from your father." A taste, a shadow of the perfected reality of communing saints.

* * * * *

Israel believed, above all else, in a God who interferes. Who comes walking in the evening and wants to know where you are. Who confused the tongues at Babel. Who arranged for Sarah's unexpected pregnancy. Who took an unwarranted liking to Nineveh. Who allowed Job to be toyed with. And who, as Christians further believe, having dabbled about in human affairs to little avail for a couple of thousand years, decided to make himself clear in Jesus Christ.

The medieval romancers, much cleverer than we at seeing connections, made stories about the Holy Rood, the cross, which originally grew untouched in Eden and was later used for the mast of Noah's ark. And at the end of the story, described in the Apocalypse of John, the tree of life, left behind so long ago in Eden, now stands in the Holy City awaiting the time when "there shall be no more curse." Thus the tree of death becomes for us the great reversal, the tree of life, long sought for but ever denied.

We are all of us somewhere on that long road that runs from the gate of Eden, closed forever to human habitation, to the gate of the New Jerusalem that stands perpetually open to receive the glory and honor of nations. And along each part of the road, wander pilgrims. A part of our journey led through Babylon, that seductive city that attempts to disguise itself as Jerusalem in order to win the allegiance of ardent seekers. But one must heed the call to come out of Babylon if one wants to journey on to the real Jerusalem.

Yet, having left Eden and Babylon behind, we still stood desolate on the road. Our Emmaus lay ahead. Moving along toward it, we too were like the disappointed disciples of a reformer, a martyred zealot, he who they had hoped "should have redeemed Israel." But the one walking beside us turns out to be, not Ché Guevara after all, but something better. Something More. Not one bound to repeat the same old patterns of power and betrayal. But one who did what we, since Eve, can never do, fully unite his will to God's.

So from Emmaus we set out once more. The road didn't end there for Cleopas and his friend, and neither does it for us. It led back to the city and in amongst the other disciples. Together we seek to build an ark for our own apocalyptic times, a community that will see us through our forty days and nights of chaos and storm, like Noah, straining our sight for the return of the dove.

```
PS          Adams, Eugenia
3551
.D35        Assault on Eden
A87x
```